King of Kings and Lord of Lords
Heralding His Soon Return

By

Kit Olsen

World Bible Society
Costa Mesa, California

King of Kings and Lord of Lords
Heralding His Soon Return

Copyright 2014 © by Kit Olsen
Email address: yeshuasfriends@yahoo.com

**Published by the World Bible Society
P.O. Box 5000, Costa Mesa. California 92628**

**First Printing July, 2014
Printed in the United States of America**

ISBN: 1940241006
ISBN-13: 9781940241005

Scripture quotations are from the Holy Bible New King James Version copyright ©1982 Thomas Nelson, Inc., the Holy Bible Authorized King James version, copyright ©1987 by Thomas Nelson, and the New American Standard Bible ©1995 Holman Bible Publishers, American Standard Bible ©1901 by Thomas Nelson & Sons.

Emboldened Scripture is added by the author for emphasis.

All of Kit Olsen's books are Scripture-based and published by the World Bible Society.

Yeshua Ha Mashiach
Jesus the Christ

The King of Kings
and
Lord of Lords

He Is the Exalted One
The Crowns He Wears
Shine Brighter
Than the Strongest
Expression of the Sun

For Chad—my special gift from heaven.
Also, for everyone who reads this book.
You are all special gifts created by the Lord.

Dedicated to all our invisible guardian angels as they steadfastly and fearlessly fight the battles for us in the heavenly realms and here on earth.

Contents

❧ Jesus Is the Word ❧

Jesus is the Word. Jesus came into the world as God in the flesh: "The Word was made flesh and dwelt among us." God became a man and dwelt among us suffering an agonizing death on the cross of Calvary to save mankind from their sins.

John 1:1-4

"IN the beginning was the Word, and the Word was with God, and the Word was God. He was in the beginning with God. All things were made through Him, and without Him nothing was made that was made.

In Him was life, and this life was the light of men. And the Word [Jesus] was made flesh and dwelt among us, and we beheld his glory as of the only begotten of the Father, full of grace and truth."

⤜ Foreword ⤛

Part One of this book is a fantasy-filled story, although much of it is based on biblical truth. Some of the characters' names are taken from Scripture, but the storyline itself is fictional with some true, prophetic events mixed in. The major biblical events woven into the text are factual. Imaginary expressions and descriptions are intended for fun and delightful reverie featuring characters from Israel, Ethiopia, and from the heavenly realm.

Our culture is drowning in the occult—New Age messages and themes, the "New Spirituality." An overwhelming number of Christian churches around the world are knowingly and unknowingly embracing teachings apart from the Word of God—the Bible, and becoming part of the apostate emergent church movement where the fundamental truths of Scripture are boldly and significantly redefined, betraying the truths of the Bible. This book is meant to counter the overwhelming, anti-biblical forces filling the minds of not only our youth, but also all those who are confused by the relentless anti-God messages imbedded in all aspects of our society throughout the world today.

Part Two is packed with serious and important information regarding salvation, spiritual deception and Christian living issues, equipping the reader to better deal with the strong pull of worldly influences that work to draw us away from the true God of the Bible. Key biblical topics including end-times Bible prophecy is touched on in a way that is easy to understand. The resource guide is a valuable tool for furthering one's spiritual growth and awareness. Some of the topics covered in this section will need parental assistance for the younger children but everything discussed is important so they can begin to be spiritually and pragmatically discerning about people and life situations.

Part One

Journey from the Land of Perfect

The Word of God Is All Powerful

"For the word of God is living and powerful, and sharper than any two-edged sword, piercing even to the division of soul and spirit, and of joints and marrow, and is a discerner of the thoughts and intents of the heart" (Hebrews 4:12).

Chapter One

Journey to Planet Earth

"Hold on Jesse, hold on! Wait for me! My foot just slipped-out of one of the stirrups," stammered Levi.

Levi's courageous horse, Shield, gently slowed down. Levi carefully wiggled his foot back into the dangling stirrup.

"Okay, that's better!" he exclaimed.

"Come on Levi," called out Jesse, "We still have to get through the Swarm of Deceit and the Maze of Lies. Hold on tight. Those nasty demons will try to knock us down."

"I'm ready!" answered Levi.

"Remember what the Lord taught us in His Scriptures; to always put on the *full* armor of God. And to keep repeating the name of Jesus Christ out loud as we ride through all the dark, dank, demon infested territories." shouted Jesse.

"Those pesky, evil creatures are everywhere. Knock them out with the Word of God!" replied Levi.

The two brave, determined angels – Angels of Intervention sent by God Himself from heaven above, six-hundred-suns and four-thousand-moons away from planet Earth navigated their way toward earth – riding their strong, limber horses through the treacherous demonic, foreboding terrain.

How the devil had corrupted the beauty of God's creation in the lower heavens. Nothing would stop these two emissaries from reaching their predestined location. The two determined angels faithfully spoke and repeated Scripture out loud – over and over, again and again. Their voices carried a melodic echo throughout the eerie, vaporous heavens as they rode with unwavering resilience to their entry point to planet Earth.

"No weapon formed against us shall prosper. Greater is He that is in me than he who is in the world. The Word of God is living and powerful and sharper than any two-edged sword."

"There they go. They're dropping down like dead flies. They're getting knocked-out like gagging roaches," exclaimed Jesse. "Keep on riding Levi!"

"Okay, okay, Jesse. The Lord has brought us through the Swarm of Deceit successfully. But hold on here come the Maze of Lies!"

"Don't look back Jesse. Don't look back," pleaded Levi. "All those demonic lies lined-up ahead are going to try to pull us down into Satan's strongholds. They want to keep us from getting to earth to help all the spiritually deceived people. So many people don't realize that Jesus is coming soon and that they need to be ready. There isn't much time left before the Rapture!"

Jesse and Levi continued their harrowing quest through the demon-plagued skies. They felt as if their journey would never end. They continued to shout-out Scriptures dodging the vicious entities determined to stop them from completing their mission. Jesse and Levi traveled with unflinching purpose giving glory to God, praising Him with these words:

The God of the Bible is the only true God.

Jesus Christ is Lord!

The God of the Bible is the only true God.

Jesus Christ is Lord!

There is no other Savior.

Only Jesus Christ can save!

There is no other Savior.

Only Jesus Christ can save!

"Aha! Watch out Levi," yelled Jesse. "Here come some more of those wretched, pathetic creatures. They're falling over and fizzling out like wobbly-kneed rag dolls."

"Okay Jesse, I'm on full alert," declared Levi, as they swiftly but cautiously rode their unfaltering horses through the murky skies.

"So Levi, we know all the so-called gods and prophets that are so popular on earth today, are really just distractions—lies that the devil uses to trick people into believing that there are many ways to heaven; a way to lure people away from the truth of the Savior—the Messiah Jesus.

We know all too well it began way back when Lucifer – the devil, rebelled and turned against God. The devil wants everyone to end up in hell with him. He is ruthless and will do anything to destroy people. He has pushed his lies into so many schools, community organizations, social clubs and religious groups – entire nations."

"You're right, Levi," replied Jesse. "We must help the people on planet Earth learn the truth about the Lord. Born-again believers—those who are faithful to the Lord Jesus are challenged every day by those who want to destroy our Lord's biblical teachings and values. Those same wicked elitists think that they are gods themselves.

The Lord God Almighty says it's very bad down there. He is grieving all the time that so many people He created never pay any attention to Him, and that multitudes even *deny* His

5

existence. Most of the world acts as if He doesn't even exist. We can't let the Lord down. We must fulfill our mission."

Don't worry Jesse, we will fulfill our mission," replied Levi. "The pagan 'New Age' gods and prophets that are widely accepted are propped up by the devil and kept adored and favored by the manipulations of demonic gangs like the Swarm of Deceit, the Maze of Lies and all the other dark forces that Satan uses to deceive the world.

Those who believe and teach that all 'paths' lead to God and heaven are unsuspecting victims of the devil's deceptions. Those who totally reject God are equally deceived. You know we can find the devil's strongholds *everywhere* in the universe. But he is very aggressively infesting planet Earth right now.

He *knows* the Lord is returning soon and that he and his demonic kingdom will be crushed, thrown into the bottomless pit, and then finally into the eternal lake of fire at the end of the one-thousand-year Millennium."

"Everything you say is true Levi, and that's why we have to get through these demonic strongholds and get to earth. Uh, oh! Keep on riding Levi. I can feel the Maze of Lies trying to pull us down. They're ganging up behind us! Don't look back. Keep on riding, Levi. Keep on riding and don't look back!" shouted Jesse. "We should be there soon."

"Don't worry Jesse, I won't look back. Look Jesse, look. Look straight ahead!" cried out Levi. "There it is. There it is. Planet Earth! Oh no. It's even worse than I imagined. It is *so* dark. It is almost completely covered with demonic lies. The Holy Spirit is weeping!

We have so much work to do and we don't have much time. The Lord says it won't be long before all the last days Scriptures are all fulfilled. Let's hurry and get to Jerusalem."

Chapter Two

Jesse and Levi Arrive in Jerusalem

The two brave angels – Angels of Intervention – faithful servants of the Lord carefully descend into the outer realms of planet Earth. Their treasured horses glide slowly as they enter the earth's atmosphere. Levi immediately bows his head and prays with conviction. "Heavenly Father, guide us now directly to Jerusalem, your beloved city. We ask this in the mighty name of Jesus. Amen."

Jesse and Levi carefully dismount from their loyal, agile horses and skillfully release them. The two radiant white stallions – sporting long, thick, plush manes quickly turn and eagerly head back toward heaven—six-hundred-suns and four-thousand-moons away from planet Earth. Then, in a split second Jesse and Levi whirl through the skies and are suddenly standing on a busy street in Jerusalem.

"We made it Jesse," whispered Levi.

Before Jesse could respond, the two angels—who now look like two very handsome sandy-haired young Jewish men, are greeted by the gentle smile of a pretty young woman, her beautiful auburn hair cascading down around her shoulders. Her bright luminous hazel eyes glisten as if reflecting the sun's golden rays. She has the love of the Lord all around her. Standing next to her is a tall, kind-faced attractive young man with a warm smile. He reaches his hand out to welcome the two newcomers.

"Shalom! Are you two new to Jerusalem? My name is Zvi, and this is my twin sister, Rachel. She had a dream last night that the Lord God, the Messiah of Israel, is going to remove all His believers in the Rapture event very soon, and that we should tell everyone we possibly can—to get ready!"

"I was reading about the Rapture in my Bible last night," added Rachel. "The Rapture is the 'catching away' to heaven of all true believers in Messiah Jesus—before the Tribulation begins. Zvi and I are Jewish believers—Hebrew Christians. We live with our family just a few minutes from here. We have a nice building where we meet together with other believers to worship our Lord—Yeshua Ha Mashiach—Jesus the Christ.

We are not popular here in Israel because so many of our people don't know that Yeshua is our Messiah. They don't want to believe it. Satan—the devil—the enemy of God has blinded their eyes and closed their hearts."

"Oh, *we* believe Yeshua is the Messiah!" said Jesse.

"My name is Jesse, and this is Levi. We *know* Yeshua is the Messiah. We are happy to meet you. We came to Jerusalem because this city is very important to the Lord. This is where He will come at the end of the Tribulation.

From here we will go to as many places as we can all over the world to warn people about the changes that are coming. We want to tell everyone about the Lord's soon return, too. We want to help people understand the truth of Yeshua. We like to call Jesus by his Hebrew name—Yeshua, especially here in Israel."

Then Levi spoke up, lamenting, "So many false teachers, religions and cults are deceiving people into thinking there is more than one true God, more than one way to heaven. Millions of people are sincerely deceived, and they don't understand the danger they are in. False religions are Satan's ultimate weapon against the true God of the Bible.

"There is only one true God, the God of the Bible and only one way to heaven, and that is through our Yeshua—the Messiah—just like the Scriptures teach. Rachel, Zvi, you know the Scriptures."

'Jesus said to him [Thomas the apostle], 'I am the way, the truth, and the life. No one comes to the Father except through me,' as written in John 14:6.

'Nor is there salvation in any other, for there is no other name under heaven given among men by which we must be saved,' as recorded in Acts 4:12.'"

"There isn't much time left before the Lord pours out His wrath during the Tribulation," exclaimed Jesse.

"Those seven years will be the most terrible years ever. I am sure you have both studied the Scriptures and know that all those who are saved, and have placed their faith in the Lord will be taken out in the Rapture to the safety of heaven before God pours out his wrath. Maybe we can all work together and warn others."

"Yes, yes. We must work together." responded Rachel.

"We would like to make some new friends who will help us get out the message that Yeshua the Messiah is coming very soon," said Levi.

"Rachel, your dream about the Rapture is right," continued Levi. "It is going to happen soon. We don't know when, but all the signs show that it is close. Yet too many people are not paying attention and will be left here on earth for the Tribulation. They will suffer terribly! Even many people who attend churches will not be taken out in the Rapture, those who are not saved; those who don't have a personal relationship with the Lord Jesus and are not truly born-again. So many churches have stopped teaching the truths of the Bible and are falling away from Christ's teachings and are creating new doctrines. No one can get into heaven without receiving Christ personally and making a commitment to Him, without asking forgiveness of their sins and also genuinely repenting.

Jesse and I have heard about some unscrupulous people, false prophets, who are trying to make a mockery of the Rapture by setting specific dates and creating media sensationalism. Then of course when the Rapture does not happen on the specified dates, the world just laughs at those of us who know the truth and are sincere. It is just another underhanded way that the devil is trying to fool people into thinking the truths of the Bible and the Rapture are just myths. May we come visit your congregation today?"

"You are welcome to come visit our congregation any time," chimed in Zvi.

"We have been involved with the ministry for many years, and especially since we finished college last year. Our father is the senior pastor and he would welcome some help with spreading the salvation message and telling others about the Rapture, the Tribulation and the Lord's Second Coming—at the end of the Tribulation. We even have a couple of extra rooms in our home church where our congregation meets. You are welcome to stay there if you don't have a place to stay yet. We'll make you feel right at home."

Jesse and Levi – the two Angels of Intervention – looked at each other winking and smiling, both thinking how no place on earth or anywhere else is even remotely close to their glorious home in heaven—six-hundred-suns and four-thousand-moons away from planet Earth.

But they eagerly and graciously accepted Zvi's offer. They were sure that the Lord had led Rachel and Zvi to them to assist with the very hard work ahead.

They all headed together to the congregation's meeting place talking amongst themselves about how they could best reach others with the Rapture message that Rachel had dreamt about. (The Rapture of all true believers is prophesied in the Holy Bible.)

The Lord Is Our Strength

Isaiah 41:28-31

"Do you not know? Have you not heard? The Everlasting God, the LORD, the Creator of the ends of the earth does not become weary or tired. His understanding is inscrutable. He gives strength to the weary, and to him who lacks might He increases power.

Though youths grow weary and tired, and vigorous young men stumble badly, yet those who wait for the LORD will gain new strength; they will mount up with wings like eagles, they will run and not get tired, they will walk and not become weary."

Ephesians 6:11-12

"Put on the whole armor of God, that you may be able to stand against the wiles of the devil. For we wrestle not against flesh and blood, but against principalities, against powers, against the rulers of the darkness of this world, against spiritual wickedness in high places."

Chapter Three

The Workers of Iniquity Discover Jesse and Levi

"**W**e have to stop them. They are going to get in our way. Something about those two feels *too heavenly* for me," simmered Darknight – a fallen angel and leader of the gang known as the Workers of Iniquity. "We'll quash them before they can start running their mouths about that Jesus of Nazareth, King of the Jews!"

"Yeah," piped in Lotto, Darknight's cohort. "We'll get them when their guard is down. Don't worry. I will keep a close watch over them."

Jesse and Levi were settling into their rooms. Eager to start their work early the next morning, they decided to get to sleep as early as possible. Even heavenly angels need a good night's sleep – that is, when they visit planet Earth. Just as they were about to fall asleep they both heard a strange, screeching sound coming from the back of the building. Jesse sat up in his bed. Levi got right up and knocked on Jesse's door.

"Open the door, Jesse. Did you hear that noise?"

"Yes, yes I did," answered Jesse.

"It's a trap," Levi exclaimed. "They know we are here. That devil is ratcheting up all his fallen angels and his demonic cohorts. They are going to try to stop us from reaching the lost souls."

"We better call out for the Lord's strengthening power so we can get through this, Levi. God is all-powerful and He will help us," whispered Jesse.

Immediately the two Angels of Intervention fell to their knees and prayed: "Father, we glorify you and praise you. We need your help so we can carry on with our mission for you here on earth. We can sense the Workers of Iniquity gang right outside our rooms. Please be with us and give us the wisdom and strength to fend them off. We ask this in Jesus' holy name. Amen."

Then it happened. The building shook and the screeching noise started up again, but much louder this time. Darknight and Lotto were gearing up for their attack against Jesse and Levi. Their robotic minions gathered behind them as they readied themselves to plunge into the building.

"They are trying to scare us—fools that they are! Those fallen angels and demons never learn. Let's let them fuss for a few minutes before we take them out," chuckled Levi.

"Ready, Jesse? Let's blast them with the Word of God!"

All of a sudden, they heard a despondent, desperate voice call out:

"Help...help!"

"It sounds like Rachel is calling for us," said Jesse.

"No. Wait. It's another trap," whispered Levi.

"It's probably Darknight, the ruthless ringleader of the Workers of Iniquity gang. The Lord warned us that he would be the first one to try to stop us from fulfilling our mission."

The voice that sounded like Rachel's voice kept calling out: "Help me, help me."

"It's definitely a trap," whispered Jesse.

Then an image that looked like Rachel appeared outside the window located toward the front of Jesse's room.

"See? It's me, Rachel. Help me. I am locked out. Please let me in, hurry."

Jesse and Levi knew exactly what was going on. The devil can appear as an "angel of light." Demons can possess people and fallen angels can manifest themselves and appear in any form that they want.

"And no wonder! For Satan himself transforms himself into an angel of light" (2 Corinthians 11:14).

The two determined Angels of Intervention stood firm staring directly at the image and said out loud the same words Jesus said to the devil when he was on earth, as recorded in Matthew 4:10:

"Away with you, Satan! For it is written, you shall worship the LORD your God, and only you shall serve."

Just as Jesse and Levi were about to quote more Scripture, they noticed, standing behind the fake image of Rachel – a small group of soldiers dressed in crisp, bright white-linen uniforms. On the front of their tunics written in bold letters were the words:

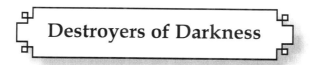

Destroyers of Darkness

Together, in unison the soldiers shouted:

We rebuke you Satan and all your demonic hordes and fallen angels, in the name of Jesus Christ – the eternal King and Savior – the Messiah of Israel and of the world!

Immediately, the image posing as Rachel melted into a life-less shriveled-up heap, falling down below onto the ground. Sure enough, it was Darknight. The crusty old fallen angel was knocked out! The rest of the demonic misfits – all the members of the Workers of Iniquity gang limped away screaming until finally the entire gang evaporated down into the earth below – gone in a flash into a pit of utter darkness. This demonic bunch was finished!

The Destroyers of Darkness, God's faithful soldiers, waved their hands toward Jesse and Levi signaling their imminent departure. They disappeared just as fast as they had appeared. This angelic army had been sent by the Lord Himself to assist Jesse and Levi in destroying the Workers of Iniquity gang. Angels helping angels wipe out the enemies of God with the living Word of God! How cool is that?

"Be of sober *spirit*, be on the alert. Your adversary, the devil, prowls around like a roaring lion, seeking someone to devour" (1 Peter 5:8).

Chapter Four

The Meeting

The next morning not a trace could be found pointing to any of the commotion that had gone on the night before with Darknight, and his miserable demonic gang. When Jesse and Levi awoke, they got right up, showered and quickly dressed for the day ahead. Refreshed and energized from the brisk splashes of water from their showers they spent some "quiet" time praying and seeking the Lord, studying their Bibles and asking Him for guidance.

After finishing their devotions, Jesse and Levi headed straight to Fellowship Hall, located next to the sanctuary – following the smell of freshly brewed coffee, home baked bread, and the delightful, unmistakable aroma of cinnamon-nut rugelach.

Zvi, Rachel and about a dozen others were already gathered together around a large, sturdy oblong wooden table sipping their morning coffee, enjoying thick chunks of wholegrain bread piled high with dollops of fresh sweet butter and swirls of strawberry jam – discussing the pressing issues of the day.

"The first thing we need to do is explain what the Rapture of the church is. Too many people confuse it with the Lord's Second Coming when every 'eye will see Him' at the very end of the Tribulation. Then we need to touch on the Tribulation, and show that it definitely happens after the Rapture. But most important, we need to present the salvation message and tie all three of these major prophesied events together in a way that can be easily understood," explained Zvi.

Jesse and Levi sat down and joined the group. Zvi looked up and said, "Please, everyone, here are our new friends, Levi and Jesse. They have come to Jerusalem to help us with the very matters we are discussing. They arrived yesterday, the morning after Rachel had her dream about the Rapture. They must have been sent directly by God!"

Everyone in the room smiled and laughed. Little did they know that Zvi's proclamation is exactly the truth! Jesse and Levi were sent to Jerusalem under the Lord's direct command, by His divine appointment—Angels of Intervention sent to alert the world that Jesus the Messiah is coming very soon.

Levi spoke right up, "Shalom! Yes, I'm Levi and this is Jesse, gesturing to his left. We are very excited to be here. We would love to get to know *all* of you very well, but because our message is urgent, especially considering the dream Rachel had the other night, Jesse and I would like to keep our total focus on moving forward with our mission.

We would like to get right out into the world and tell as many people as possible that they must get ready for the Rapture of the church—or they will not be taken up when the Lord descends from heaven with a shout—with the voice of the archangel, and with the trumpet of God, when He calls all true believers home to heaven at the last trump as taught in 1 Thessalonians 4:16-17. In 1 Corinthians 15:52, Scripture tells us that the immortal bodies of all believers will be changed, when the last trump sounds, 'in the twinkling of an eye' into new glorified bodies like Jesus has.

Sadly, some people confuse the last trump the apostle Paul spoke of in 1 Corinthians with the same trumpets spoken of in Joel 2:1, Matthew 24:31, and Revelation 11:15-18, and think that believers will have to go through at least half of the Tribulation. But we must remind those people that John wrote Revelation about forty years *after* Paul wrote his first epistle to the Corinthians, and that Paul could not have been making reference to an event that had not yet been revealed."

"We agree," said Rachel. "Your points about the Rapture of the church are right, Levi. We also agree that in order to keep our full focus on the task at hand, we will consider each other, our entire group here – brothers and sisters in the Lord and work together as closely as we can. We will have plenty of time to get to know each other more personally in the future."

"Yes, after all, we do have all of eternity to spend together. We have all of eternity together, and all of eternity with our Savior, the Lord God Almighty, the Creator of heaven and earth!" exclaimed Zvi with great gusto and enthusiasm.

"Our soon coming King, our soon coming King!" cheered the happy group.

"Okay!" exclaimed Rachel. "My father, Pastor Hezzie will now lead us in prayer and then we will get on with figuring out our plan of action."

Pastor Hezzie stood up to pray, asking the others to stand with him. "Father God, we come before you on this special day. We thank you for bringing all of us together. We praise you. We ask you to guide us and protect us from evil as we organize ourselves to go out into the world and tell others about your Son's soon return. Please give us courage, and wisdom. We thank you and honor you and we ask this in the holy name of Yeshua, the Savior of mankind. Amen."

And everyone said, "Amen!"

"Alright!" said Pastor Hezzie. Let's break-up into two groups. I have a list of ideas we can use to put together a plan of action. Zvi, Rachel – you go with our two new friends Jesse and Levi – and work from this list. The rest of us will do some research on the Internet to find the communities that need to hear our message the most. But I'm afraid that list is going to be longer than we can handle."

"We'll do all we can to reach as many people as possible," said Levi. We have had a lot of experience witnessing to people. Let's trust the Lord to guide us!"

Many hours passed as the dedicated group worked together to come up with a plan of action on how to reach others for Christ and spread the word about the Rapture, which takes place before the Tribulation. It was well past noon when a cheerful, concerned voice of a young boy, asked: "Aren't you all hungry? Mom says you should all come over to our house and have a late lunch."

"And who is this charming, young man? Where did you come from?" asked Jesse.

Rachel leapt up from her chair and answered, "This is our little brother, Yossi."

She gave him a big hug, lifting him up just a bit off the floor. His dark, wavy brown hair flopped past the back of his shirt collar. When Rachel sat back down, Yossi remained standing and addressed the group.

"I am twelve years old!" exclaimed Yossi. "I'm *almost* a teenager. Some people think I am a computer genius. I'm learning how to do PHP, Sequel, Auto CAD, Photoshop, Illustrator, Flash MX, Paint Shop Pro and Word Press – stuff like that. I can do some programs like BinEdit 2.2.8, ZModeler v1.07B, ZModeler 2, gMax, Dreamweaver, Fireworks, and mobile apps. I also like to film videos with my favorite hand-held video camera.

I edit all my videos on my computer and write stories about most of them. I am *almost* old enough to have my very own, exceptionally produced, YouTube channel – supervised by my parents of course. We only had a half-day of school today. It's the first day of our spring vacation!"

After young Yossi finished speaking everyone in the room simultaneously burst into loud hearty, warm-hearted laughter—delightfully surprised by the unexpected, captivating entertainment delivered by this very charming young orator. His impassioned, highly energetic delivery enhanced his already descriptive monologue.

"I'll be sure to ask you for help next time I have a problem with a computer project." said Jesse. "Me too!" piped in Levi.

Levi and Jesse would soon find out just how helpful Yossi would be.

"Okay everyone," said Pastor Hezzie. "Let's go have some lunch. We can discuss our progress on our project while we eat."

Sharing Ideas at Lunch

"Come in, come in, lunch is ready!" motioned Sarah as she opened the door. "Hey everyone, this is my wonderful mother, Sarah," said Rachel. "She is the best cook in the whole world. You will love the specialties that she has prepared for us."

"I'm pleased to meet all of you. Please come in. Come in and make yourselves comfortable at the table – here in our dining room. I hope you all like falafel, Israeli hummus and couscous. Oh, and I made some delicious red lentil stew. Jacob's mother taught me how to make it with her special Ethiopian touch. I am sure you will meet Jacob and his family while you are visiting. They are part of our congregation, Jewish believers who came to faith in our Messiah when they first visited our church.

Ah! And we have cherry blintzes and Yossi's favorite apple cake, and freshly picked grapes from our vineyard for dessert. We have plenty, so please help yourselves to as much as you like," announced Sarah with a big, loving smile.

The hungry group happily sat together enjoying the delicious delicacies that Sarah had prepared. Magnificent aromas of home-cooked food permeated throughout the entire house. The air was buzzing with voices of delight as the companions devoured their lunches.

"This is really delicious," said Levi.

"It's great! I'm ready for seconds," beamed Jesse.

Yossi was busily eating his lunch and had been very silent. Then, when the others were quieting down a bit he said, "I have been listening to all of you talk about the best way to reach people – how to tell them about our Lord Yeshua. I have a couple of ideas."

"Alright, Yossi, we would like to hear your ideas," his father responded.

"Well, since I don't have school for two weeks, I could help you accelerate the project. I have some friends who are really good with their computers, too. We can develop a couple of special software programs you could use to send out the salvation message and any other information you want that has to do with the Lord and His Scriptures. We can contact all the schools, businesses, and homes. In fact I think we could send whatever we want to nearly everyone on earth," suggested Yossi.

"Now that sounds like a huge undertaking," pondered Yossi's dad.

"Don't worry, Dad. I have a very friendly relationship with our Messiah. I pray a lot every day. I read my Bible and study the Holy Scriptures. I am sure He will show me a way to do this. He is my Heavenly Father and I know He will listen to and answer my prayer when I ask Him to help me with the project."

"Can you be more specific Yossi?" asked Levi.

"Yes, well, you all know television is not as popular as it used to be, although we don't want to leave it out.

Everyone, it seems, likes to use cell phones – smartphones and computers for communication, for news, advertising, and to access fun social media sites like Twitter and Facebook. And the microblogs like Tumir and Pheed. Messaging services are available—Kik, WhatsaApp still mostly in the U.S., WeChat in China, KakaoTalk in Korea and Line here in the Middle East and Asia. We can also access Instagram and Snapchat.

We'll come up with a strong program that will get our message directly to all those sources. I have been reading a lot about how that all works. With the help of some of my friends and with Yeshua's guidance, I think we can come up with some great stuff. You know Levi – we Israeli's are known for our advanced technological skills."

"You are a very cool kid, Yossi," said Levi. "I think you are on to something. When can you show us a sample of what you have in mind?"

"Well, let's see, maybe by Tuesday. It's Friday today and I'll need at least a few days to work on this. It should be a lot of fun. I'll get started right away, that is if it's all right with you, Dad," Yossi looked to his father.

"You have my blessing, Yossi. I can see how the Lord has given you a sharp creative mind, and you want to use it to His glory. Yossi, you are honoring the Lord by being mindful of the Scripture in Ecclesiastes: 'Remember now your Creator in the days of your youth.' I am proud to call you my son!"

Chapter Five

Yossi and His Friends Get to Work
And Rachel Has another Dream

Immediately after the lunch festivities ended, Yossi hurried to telephone his best buddy, Eli. Eli immediately recognized Yossi's talents with computers when they met at an advanced computer seminar at summer camp a couple of years back. They became good friends very quickly. It doesn't matter that Yossi is twelve, and that Eli is sixteen.

Yossi is a very mature, likeable kid. He makes friends easily because he is very outgoing, attentive and always helps others whenever he can. He smiles a lot and always tells people how great God is. Yossi and Eli have a common bond with their talents for computers, but their greatest bond is their mutual love for the true biblical Jesus – that is what makes their friendship great.

"Let's all meet over here at my house tonight, Eli. Tell everyone to bring laptops and phones. Yes, Jacob and Peter. We have a lot of work ahead of us, lots of research. Better tell them to bring their sleeping bags too, and get permission to stay overnight. I think we are going to be up very late," exclaimed Yossi with great excitement.

"Yes, I already checked everything with my parents. They said we should do whatever we need to for the next few days while we are working on this project.

And yes, we have plenty of bandwidth over here to handle anything we need to do. And Eli, can you stop at Malek's Bakery before they close for the Sabbath, and pick-up some snacks for us? And be sure to get something Jacob likes. He is still adjusting to our Israeli food since he and his family arrived here from Ethiopia. He's amazingly advanced in his computer skills, but even after so many years he is still slow to sample some of our special foods."

"That goes without saying, Yossi," answered Eli. "I'll bring lots of good stuff. And don't worry. I know what Jacob likes: The hummus, the crusty thick wholegrain bagels and the sweet noodle kugle. I'll drive by and get him and Peter, and we'll see you later tonight."

Yossi, his family and friends were not strict observers of Jewish holidays like Shabbat, but they did enjoy celebrating some of those special days on occasion. The Bible teaches that we should rest one day a week – some people rest on Saturday and others on Sunday. The most important thing is that we worship the Lord every day.

As soon as Eli and the others arrived at Yossi's house, they discussed how they all felt that God had called them together to work on their assignments. They agreed that they would ask the Lord for special blessings, and promised each other to use the days ahead all for His glory. With great determination the boys settled into the spacious game room upstairs, now officially dubbed: "Project Headquarters." The boys started immediately to forge ahead with their work.

Gathered together in a circle in the expansive game room, they clasped each other's hands and respectfully bowed their heads in reverence to the good Lord. Eli, the eldest in the group led the dedicated boys in prayer.

"Our great and faithful Father, God of Abraham, Isaac and Jacob, we thank you for honoring us with this assignment. Please help us to work together with wisdom and clarity. We know time is short before you take us home in the Rapture. Give us the answers we need so we can do everything possible to reach others before it's too late, and they are left on earth to suffer through the Tribulation. Quicken our spirits and lead us as we get to work for you. In Yeshua's name, we pray."

And all four boys shouted, "Amen!"

"Okay, everybody, let's write out the salvation message and the Rapture/Tribulation warning using the notes from the meeting my dad had with the others earlier today. We'll use the rest of those notes as an outline for what else we need to do. And let's get our technical juices flowing. Let's get the show on the road!" shouted Yossi.

Meanwhile, Yossi's parents, Hezzie and Sarah, were downstairs in the family room studying the Holy Scriptures. "It sounds like they are off to a good start up there," said Pastor Hezzie.

"I wonder if they will get any sleep. They are all so dedicated to the Lord and eager to work on this project. How blessed we are," Sarah happily remarked.

"We have worked very hard with our children. Rachel and Zvi are great examples of living their faith and they have had a strong influence over their little brother. But Sarah, I thank God for *you*, for your faithful devotion to our family and most of all your devotion to the Lord. Without your patience and loving guidance who knows how the kids would have turned out," said Hezzie.

"Oh, Hezzie, you have been a great, very positive influence on our children. They admire you and your tremendous love for our Messiah," responded Sarah.

"Yes, that is true, but it is your sacrifice to be at home and put aside your medical career so the children could have the stability of your being here for them is what has really made the difference. Too many people underestimate how important a mother's love and presence is in the home. I think that is one major reason there are so many problems in families and with the world in general," said Hezzie.

"Once Zvi and Rachel were born, I knew that my career had to be placed aside," replied Sarah. Being available to our children is much more important to me than trying to prove to the world that I can be a 'successful' career woman and make additional income so we can have the latest popular car or boat in our driveway – or keep up with the popular fashion trends. My success is my family. The Lord has honored my decision to put our children first. He has certainly blessed us. How grateful I am.

We also know that the devil wants parents to have a less positive influence over their children, so that they will become rebellious, get into trouble and stray from the Lord. He has been working overtime to corrupt the world and make it difficult for families to live on one income. Satan has filled the minds of so many with greed. Families are under attack like never before.

Many moms would love to stay home with their children but they must work to help pay the bills. I'm sure those moms put their children first in their hearts and love them very much, but they simply have less time to spend with their kids.

I have seen situations where families become even closer under those conditions. So the devil's plan to try to destroy the family does not always succeed. Only the Lord can fix these problems," sighed Sarah. "And He will Hezzie, when He returns to rule and reign at the end of the Tribulation."

"All the more reason to have strong faith and to trust in the Lord—to diligently seek Him each and every day," pondered Hezzie, as he turned the pages of his Bible.

"Every morning I read my favorite passage from Hebrews, verse 11:6. Here, it is." Hezzi pointed his finger to the Scripture.

Together Hezzie and Sarah read the verse out loud: "But without faith it is impossible to please *Him*, for he who comes to God must believe that He is, and that He is a rewarder of those who diligently seek Him."

"I think the Lord has blessed us because He knows that our hearts are totally devoted to Him, and that we sincerely and faithfully do seek Him," said Hezzie.

"We have had our challenges, but the Lord has never failed us or let us down. Although, sometimes we have had to be very patient waiting for some answers to prayer—but God's timing is not ours, and that is where faith and trust come in."

"We better get some sleep Hezzie," remarked Sarah, holding back a yawn. "It has been a long, wonderful day. I can hear Rachel and Zvi upstairs both getting ready to get some sleep. I think Yossi and his friends will be up late, working. May the Lord bless them and guide them as they give their time and allegiance to Him so selflessly."

Pastor Hezzi, Sarah, Zvi and Rachel all settled into their beds for the night. Yossi, Eli, Peter and Jacob all continued to quietly work into the early morning. Rachel fell asleep quickly, worn out from all the excitement of the past few days. Her bedroom was a very special and peaceful place. She considered it her private getaway where she prayed, studied her cherished Bible, relaxed and daydreamed. She affectionately called her room: Hideaway Willow.

Immediately, she began to have an unusually vivid dream. She saw herself being carried-up high in the sky in the arms of two stunningly handsome golden-bronze angels with glimmering almond-colored eyes. Their statuesque strong, thin frames draped in long billowing white gossamer garments that seemed to have a life of their own. Rachel noticed a huge golden sign on her way up. It read:

Heaven - The Land of Perfect - Straight Ahead

The Land of Perfect, six-hundred-suns and four-thousand-moons away from planet Earth is the most magnificent place where *anything* is possible. It is the most holy and pure place where only the love of God rules. It is the most powerful place—it holds together all the other galaxies. Everything in The Land of Perfect is totally pure.

As Rachel slept, her guardian angel, the leader of all the angels in Hideaway Willow, began to watch over her with careful devotion as Rachel's lips slowly formed into a beautiful, tranquil smile. Then some soft quiet tears gently flowed from her slumbering eyes. The tears slowly streamed down the cheeks of her delicate face. Rachel's guardian angel wondered what she could be dreaming about, to cause a smile on her face and tears at the same time.

It seemed that Rachel was undergoing a consecrated revelation of splendor! She was seeing magnificent lifelike scenes of heaven; as if she were right there—six-hundred-suns and four-thousand-moons away from planet Earth.

Rachel happily observed what seemed to be endless miles of breathtaking, stunning, glorious – indescribable beauty, while experiencing unfathomable joy and tranquility. Rich lustrous green grass, greener than she had ever seen and flowers made of brilliant shades of yellow, lavender and blue, and other colors she had never seen before; lakes that shimmered like sparkling translucent aqua-blue glass. Everything had extraordinary life-like brilliance, unlike anything anywhere on planet Earth. Peace and serenity permeated everywhere at every moment.

All of heaven was filled with an overwhelming love for the Lord. Every tree and every flower, and all the heavenly animals seemed to be filled with the joy and presence of the Lord. The tears Rachel shed as she slept were tears of joy. In her dream state, Rachel longed to be home forever, in heaven, The Land of Perfect, with the Lord—whose glory filled every inch of the atmosphere. A euphoric serenity surrounded all of heaven and the melodious prayers of God's holy angels could be heard continuously worshipping the Lord with majestic praise.

As she slept, Rachel observed that every time a flower swayed from the breeze, powerful thoughts of love surged into the air throughout all of heaven. The all-encompassing love of the living God seemed to flow into and throughout everything. The trees were like healing balms of love and joy, expressing the abundant compassion and mercy of the Lord. It seemed that with all the glory that could be relegated from heaven above, Rachel was being prepared for a most wondrous, miraculous event – the catching up of all believers on earth to their homes in heaven – in the coming Rapture.

The certainty of the Rapture was confirmed to her again, with much more intensity than in the dream she had a few nights before. This dream of heaven was just a taste of what her future would be like. She saw rivers that looked like ethereal healing channels used to keep everyone healthy and young. She saw snow that fell, but didn't. Snow that was there but wasn't! Snow that would fall to the ground but wasn't there at all! She saw miraculous, magnificent views of wonderful, playful, supernatural occurrences not possible on earth.

And the exquisite music! Rachel had never heard anything like it before. Thousands and thousands of angelic voices were singing, praising God. It was the most soothing sound she had ever heard, touching the very depths of her soul. Time seemed to stand still and everywhere she looked there was goodness and mercy coming from God's Throne Room.

After a while, as Rachel continued to sleep, the Lord showed Rachel's guardian angel some of the dream, the part about the Rapture. Exhilarated by the exciting news, Rachel's guardian angel summoned all the angels assigned by God to watch over Hideaway Willow. She made an announcement about the soon coming glorious Rapture event. A very energetic fun-loving group of ivory-pale angels appeared nearly instantly, respectfully surrounding the sleeping Rachel.

They looked at her with pure love and joyous delight. As Rachel continued to sleep—totally enthralled by her spectacular dream, the cheerful angels began to celebrate, rejoicing and singing—elated by the happy news of the coming Rapture miracle. Finally, all those who belong to the Lord would be taken to heaven one day soon, freed from the hardships of earthly life and protected from the wrath that would fall upon planet Earth during the Tribulation years.

Surely the special Council of Miracle Workers in heaven must have had something to do with God giving Rachel such an important dream. They must have done something very special for the Lord! The angels danced and laughed, creating so much fun-loving mischief, noise and ruckus that Rachel's guardian angel had to repeatedly "hush" the group.

Even the angel's harps began strumming themselves, and without the assistance of the music angels! The flutes were humming, and the younger angels in the group danced enthusiastically to a steady hip-hop sound, and a progressive reggae-funk beat. ♫

A full-fledged party was in fact going on inside the walls of Hideaway Willow – Rachel's special getaway, where in her dream-state she was given a glimpse of heaven—the Land of Perfect, six-hundred-suns and four-thousand-moons away from planet Earth.

It was now about 3:00 a.m. Yossi and his friends were just about ready to call it a day...

"That's it Eli, that is it! We can gain a lot of good ground integrating these two programs. I think we have made a great start. We all better get some sleep, so we can keep working all day tomorrow," exclaimed Yossi. "I am feeling really tired."

"Peter, Jacob, you are both terrific researchers. We've made a lot of progress. We have about two weeks to perfect this idea and then we can hand everything over to Levi and Jesse, who seem to be very knowledgeable about so many things. At the meeting with my dad yesterday, they seemed to have an unusual ability to comprehend everything very quickly.

Have you all noticed how they can calculate and add up numbers in their heads in no time? They are so smart! My dad noticed that about them right away. There is something really special and out of the ordinary about those two, but my dad says he can't quite figure out what it is."

"I have noticed how they seem to know so much about any topic," added Peter. "They are both kind of like walking encyclopedias."

"Shhh...quiet you guys!" admonished Eli. "Did you hear that?" Yossi looked at his three friends and said, "I thought I heard singing and the sound of some flutes and harps coming from Rachel's room. I must be very tired."

Chapter Six

Getting Ready to Reach the World for Jesus the Messiah

Matthew 28:19

"Go therefore and make disciples of all the nations, baptizing them in the name of the Father and the Son and the Holy Spirit."

The days passed quickly as Yossi, Eli, Peter and Jacob spent every waking moment working on their project – perfecting the new software programs they were creating and tending to every detail related to their contribution to the evangelical project.

Jesse and Levi worked with Rachel, Zvi and Pastor Hezzie over at Fellowship Hall with some volunteers. Everyone was especially enthused because of Rachel's latest dream. Levi asked her to try to relate some of it.

"Everything was breathtakingly beautiful in the dream – a place of exquisite perfection!" related Rachel. "It was a serious dream but a very fun-loving one too, with what seemed to be a bit of whimsical fantasy. We can't be sure what heaven is really like except for what we read in Scripture.

I think my imagination was tied into the dream, but I am sure the part about the soon coming Rapture is very true. I think we should do everything we can to spread the salvation message and warn others about the coming Tribulation."

"Yes, I think you are right," said Levi. The Lord wants no one to perish and for all to come to repentance. It grieves Him to think that there are still so many people who want nothing to do with Him. Television shows, the Internet, sports, personal hobbies and social events seem to be 'god' for so many people. The Lord wants people to enjoy life, but too many people don't realize that it is God Himself who makes it possible for us to do anything at all.

Instead, people ignore Him. And who knows Rachel, maybe some of those fantasy-like things you saw and experienced in your dream are really what heaven is like," continued Levi, winking at Jesse.

"You know we have a great God and He can do anything at all! He is the great 'I AM,' the Alpha and Omega – the Beginning and the End, the First and the Last."

"I say Amen to that." declared Pastor Hezzie. "Rachel, I am sure your dream was another confirmation that we should work as quickly as possible and reach as many people as we can, before it is too late. I think Yossi and his friends will be coming over this afternoon to share their strategies for our reach-out witnessing campaign. In the meantime, let's all go over our notes."

Just as Pastor Hezzie finished talking, Yossi and his crew walked into Fellowship Hall.

"Shalom, Dad, shalom, everybody," said Yossi, with a big grin on his face. "We are ready to show all of you what we have been working on over the past few days. Is this a good time?"

"Your timing is perfect," replied Pastor Hezzie.

"We are anxious to get our message to the world and reach as many people as possible," added Jesse.

"We have a plan of action!" responded Yossi.

"We have worked hard to get everything working smoothly, and it looks like we have found some dedicated believers in every country in the world committed to steadily work together with us. Peter and Jacob have spent a great deal of time and effort recruiting representatives who will work closely with our ministry," explained Yossi.

"Representatives located in every country in the world? Wow, that is amazing," remarked Zvi.

"We have been busy developing software programs that will make it very easy for everyone involved with our ministry to keep in touch with each other," continued Yossi.

"We are also developing software programs that will get our message out to as many people as possible. We are figuring out some good ways to send out inviting messages in the form of advertisements to every smartphone.

We will plan to place ads on all major Web hosting sites and search engines. We will create ads offering a 'Free Gift.' And that 'free gift' is salvation thru Yeshua, the Messiah! A clever way to get someone to click on our link so we can share the salvation message, but we will also mention that so much of what is going on in the world today was foretold by prophets of old in the Bible, and Yeshua Himself.

We will then give a warning about the Tribulation and how no one has to go through it if they get saved—if they genuinely accept Yeshua as their Savior, repent and make Him Lord of their lives.

Then we will explain the Rapture. Peter is working on some exciting flash type ads that will especially catch the attention of younger folks like us. Eli and Jacob are refining a program that will place our ads on the front pages of all search engines and Web hosting sites.

In the ads, we will also include a list of current events that relate to prophetic Scriptures. Eli, Peter, Jacob and I will update the list every day after school. We will have a call in phone number that anyone can reach immediately simply by clicking on it, in case they have any questions or want to tell us that they made a decision to accept Christ and receive prayer and guidance.

This is where all our representatives worldwide will be a huge help. We'll give you more of the details on how that will work, soon. We also have a television campaign in the works, but our greatest focus will be to keep the new website we are working on, updated.

We can add any downloads we want making them available on the Internet as well as on smartphones. Most people are attached to their phones day and night!

Like I said before, we are creating a new, very inviting website for the campaign, a really good looking one—very user friendly. We would like to call it: 'Get Ready – Jesus Is Coming Soon!'

Eli will be in charge of keeping the website current. We can add any downloads we choose at any time onto the site – like the Bible tracts that Jesse and Levi are developing, or any- thing like that.

We will have the entire salvation message on the website, and detailed explanations about the Rapture and the Tribulation, and the Second Coming presented with some nice graphics and attractive illustrations.

So that's it for now. Our report today is to let you all know that we are well on our way to getting our message out there!" exclaimed Yossi.

"This all sounds very promising." said Pastor Hezzie. "We will need to organize ourselves very carefully making the best use of our time. As soon as you have all your ideas ready to put into motion, we will all sit down together and clarify all of our roles."

"We should be ready in a few more days," responded Eli.

"Great!" called out Levi. "In the meantime we will keep producing hard copies of our tracts that present our message. I know most people have become very dependent on their phones and computers, but there are still those who are not and we need to reach those folks, too. We have learned about some believers who work specifically for companies that distribute mass mailings throughout the world – with their help we can reach a lot of people in that way."

"What about the third-world nations where only the rich and powerful elitists have access to computers and cell phones, and mail is not delivered regularly?" asked Rachel, as she stood up and stretched her arms.

"Not to worry, Rachel," replied Jesse. "Levi and I have that part of the world covered. We have been in touch with many missionaries who are more than eager to help us any way they can. They are already doing a good job on their own, but they are very glad to be getting some assistance. You leave that part up to us."

"What about China, North Korea, and the many other countries that have dictatorships? It is not safe for people in those places to even own a Bible," continued Rachel.

"You leave those countries up to Jesse and me, Rachel. We will find a way to get to those who are living under oppressive rulers. We already have undercover agents for the Lord covertly spreading the salvation message in many places like that. I heard about a Bible teacher from a big Bible organization in the USA who some years ago snuck Bible templates into Russia and printed thousands of Bibles on the communist presses.

Somehow he convinced those in charge that they were there to do a massive upgrade on the printing presses—which they did during the day—but at night he and his small group of workers were covertly printing out and binding Bibles and delivering them to underground home churches all over Russia with the help of dedicated Russian believers.

Hundreds of brave believers have underground churches right in their homes in many countries where the governments are godless and against the faith. We will find a way to get our message about the soon coming Rapture to everyone. Just trust the Lord, He will show us the way," asserted Levi.

"But hold on everybody," exclaimed Zvi. What about all the different languages? How can we possibly reach so many people when they speak so many different languages?"

Eli spoke right up. "That is something we are working on with the computer software we are developing. We will be able to quickly translate our information from English or Hebrew into any language. Although the many tribes in some of the African countries speak so many languages that I don't think we can cover all them.

We will carefully list translations for the most predominant languages in those nations, and trust the Lord that all the tribes will be reached by interpreters who are friendly with the missionaries that Jesse and Levi are connected with."

"Amazing!" replied Zvi.

"We better get back to the game room at my house – to our Project Headquarters and continue working," asserted Yossi.

"Thank you, for putting so much effort into this very important project, everyone. The Lord will bless you!" called out Pastor Hezzie.

Everyone in the room quickly and quietly got back to work preparing whatever was necessary to launch the witnessing campaign to alert the world about the Rapture, the Tribulation and the Second Coming of the Lord Jesus.

"Whatever you do, do your work heartily, as for the Lord rather than for men, knowing that from the Lord you will receive the reward of the inheritance. It is the Lord Christ whom you serve" (Colossians 3:23-24).

Security of the One Who Trusts in the Lord

Psalm 91:1-16

"He who dwells in the secret place of the Most High shall abide under the shadow of the Almighty. I will say of the Lord, *'He is* my refuge and my fortress; my God, in Him I will trust.'

Surely He shall deliver you from the snare of the fowler *and* from the perilous pestilence. He shall cover you with His feathers, and under His wings you shall take refuge; His truth *shall be your* shield and buckler.

You shall not be afraid of the terror by night, *nor* of the arrow *that* flies by day, *nor* of the pestilence *that* walks in darkness, *Nor* of the destruction *that* lays waste at noonday. A thousand may fall at your side, and ten thousand at your right hand; *but* it shall not come near you. Only with your eyes shall you look, and see the reward of the wicked.

Because you have made the LORD, *who is* my refuge, *even* the Most High, your dwelling place, no evil shall befall you, nor shall any plague come near your dwelling; for He shall give His angels charge over you, to keep you in all your ways. In *their* hands they shall bear you up, lest you dash your foot against a stone. You shall tread upon the lion and the cobra, the young lion and the serpent you shall trample underfoot.

'Because he has set his love upon Me, therefore I will deliver him; I will set him on high, because he has known My name. He shall call upon Me, and I will answer him; I *will be* with him in trouble; I will deliver him and honor him. With long life I will satisfy him, and show him My salvation.'"

Chapter Seven

Yossi and His Friends Are Challenged

2 Corinthians 10:3-4

"For though we walk in the flesh, we do not war according to the flesh. For the weapons of our warfare *are* not carnal but mighty in God for pulling down strongholds."

"Something is interfering with my computer," said Eli.

"What do you mean?" asked Peter.

"I'm not sure. I am checking to see if my computer has a virus, but everything is coming up normal," replied Eli.

"Watch this, everybody. Every time I try to key in one of the codes for our new program my computer freezes up. I just had it serviced and everything has been in perfect working order, except suddenly now, and for no good reason—I am having this weird crashing glitch," explained Eli.

"Hey, I seem to be having the same problem," said Yossi.

"Me too," said Jacob.

The three boys looked over at Peter.

"What about you?"

"Yes, my computer is freezing up now too, and my keyboard is typing words backwards whenever I try to type. Something very strange is going on," responded Peter.

Around the same time the guys were experiencing major problems with their computers, Jesse and Levi over at Fellowship

Hall were suddenly getting a very odd feeling that they should go check on Yossi and his group. When they arrived at the house, Sarah cheerfully pointed them upstairs. Levi knocked on the door.

"Hey guys!" said Jesse. "It's Levi and Jesse. Is everything all right in there?

"Come on in," said Yossi. "Please close the door. Actually, we are having some very strange computer problems that don't make any sense."

Jesse and Levi looked at one another. They sensed a demonic undercurrent, a very strong one.

"You know everyone; we *are* living in a spiritual battlefield. The devil and his demonic forces are always working to disrupt and destroy the lives of people. And when it comes to those who are on the Lord's side, you can be sure evil forces will try to cause trouble for them. They will do anything and everything to try to stop the Lord's work. Do you mind if we try to help with this problem?" asked Levi.

"Please do!" replied Eli.

Levi and Jesse dropped down to the floor, onto their knees.

"Come on guys – join in, we need to pray, right now," declared Levi.

The four boys approached Levi and Jesse, taking their positions next to one another on their knees, giving reverence to the Lord.

Heavenly Father, said Jesse. "You know exactly what is going on here. We rebuke the devil in the name of Jesus of Nazareth, the Almighty King. Please help us. We sense the enemy trying to stop us from moving forward. Please do whatever it takes to resolve this problem. Give us wisdom and courage. In Yeshua's name, we pray. Amen."

"Levi and I will check your computers. Stay here on this side of the room," said Jesse.

The group of concerned computer buffs quietly sat on large comfortable cushioned chairs while Jesse and Levi checked all the computers.

"We are going to have to call in some reinforcements," said Jesse.

"What do you mean?" asked Yossi.

"Well, you see, we are going to ask some of our friends to help us. There is a very nasty demonic stronghold over all your computers," declared Levi.

Without warning, there was a knock on the door. It was Yossi's mom, Sarah.

"Jesse, Levi – there are two very nice, friendly gentlemen downstairs. They say you asked them to come by to check on how the project is going."

"Oh, yes, yes," answered Levi. "Please ask them to come up."

As soon as the two energetic men entered the game room, the room seemed to light up a bit.

"These are our friends, Michael, and Gabriel," said Jesse. "We've known them for a very long time."

Michael and Gabriel were wearing what looked like white military uniforms. On the front of their shirts across the front pockets, embroidered in small golden letters were the words:

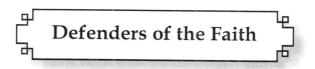

Defenders of the Faith

"Nice to meet you, shalom!" said Yossi. "Where are you guys from?"

"Oh, well, uh – we came to visit Jesse and Levi from our home. We heard you are having some computer problems and that you are all working on a very important project for the Lord God Almighty!" answered Gabriel.

"Yes, we are under demonic attack," said Eli.

"When doing the Lord's work, it is not unusual to be attacked by the enemy. We will do everything we can to help," said Michael.

"Levi, Jesse, I think it would be a good idea if we had a little space to work on this," related Michael.

"Oh yes, of course. We'll take a break and go over to Fellowship Hall and see what is going on over there. Come on guys, let's let Michael and Gabriel work on this situation for a while," said Jesse.

As soon as everyone left the game room, Michael and Gabriel—God's angels sent directly from heaven, four-hundred-suns and two-thousand-moons away from planet Earth, fell to their knees and began to pray. Gabriel prayed along silently; Michael prayed out loud:

"Father God, our mighty King, you sent us here so quickly on this emergency mission. We understand the entire project is in serious jeopardy. We do not want to alarm the young boys who have worked so hard for you. They are on the verge of losing total ability to go forward with this mission. The enemy is very crafty and has frozen all-lines of communication needed to complete this project. Strengthen us and give us breakthrough spiritual strength to ward off, and totally destroy all these vicious satanic strongholds. We ask this in the glorious and mighty name of Jesus Christ. Amen."

"So Gabriel, we know that Satan, the devil, has made all forms of media his fortress for a very long time now," pondered Michael. "He is the 'prince of the power of the air' as the Scriptures teach. Scripture also teaches he is the 'father of lies.' It is evident from the occult influence and moral decline found in so many movies, videos, books, magazines, computer games, the Internet, television, music, the entertainment industry in general, that this world is very heavily under Satan's domain.

He is especially deceptive and cunning when it comes to all educational tools, like books and entertainment aimed at children and young people. He is an expert at making evil look good. Tragically, millions of parents are fooled because they don't know the Scriptures. Their children are being pulled away from things of the Lord and pulled into the devil's clutches. And it is all so 'politically correct' thanks to corrupt leaders and politicians.

Thousands of years ago the apostle Paul wrote in the book of Ephesians in the second chapter, the first and second verses about how the devil controls the areas communication. He has succeeded in polluting millions of minds, and has plenty of demonic help to destroy even more.

'And you He made alive, who were dead in trespasses and sins, in which you once walked according to the course of this world, according to the prince of the power of the air, the spirit who now works in the sons of disobedience.'

And this is what Jesus said about the devil," continued Michael:

"He was a murderer from the beginning, and does not stand in the truth because there is no truth in him. Whenever he speaks a lie, he speaks from his own nature, for he is a liar and the father of lies. The apostle John wrote that in the book of John in the eighth chapter, the forty forth verse."

"The prophet Isaiah also warned about evil in Isaiah 5:20," added Gabriel.

"'Woe to those who call evil good and good evil; who substitute darkness for light and light for darkness; who substitute bitter for sweet, and sweet for bitter!'"

"We have to pull out all the heavy artillery," responded Michael. "I think we should remind that old devil, the serpent just WHO is in charge!"

"Alright, we'll do whatever we have to. God is with us. He is in charge!" answered Gabriel.

"Are you ready?" asked Michael

"I'm ready!" exclaimed Gabriel.

"You know, it's just a bit too quiet in here, be careful," whispered Michael.

The two angels closed their eyes. Just as they were about to pray again, the entire room went dark. Strange sizzling sounds started to come from the computers. A hissing sound – like that of an attacking rattlesnake began to pulse throughout the room. The light came back on but kept fluttering. Everything looked distorted. A tall human-like image with glaring yellow eyes, wearing dark skin-tight clothes unexpectedly appeared in front of the two angels. It had no nose, and only a straight slit for a mouth.

Then, in an instant the image turned into a young, sweetly smiling beautiful woman with lustrous golden hair, and then morphed into a jet-black wildcat with huge piercing yellow-green eyes. It opened its large mouth showing its sharp, chiseled teeth. It arched its back as if ready to pounce. Michael and Gabriel immediately began to pray.

"Satan, you have no authority over us. We plead the blood of Jesus over this household, over this entire project, and anyone and everything involved with it. You have no hold over us, over this ministry, over this project. We rebuke you in the name of Yeshua Ha Mashiach, Jesus the Christ. You are already defeated and we order you in the name of Jesus of Nazareth to return to your demonic dimension in the atmosphere. We demand that you retreat in the name of the Savior, Jesus Christ the Lord. Amen."

The large black wildcat let out a wounded, agonizing sound. Its body quivered, dropping hard to the ground. It growled and hissed, struggling – trying to get back up.

"Satan, you remember us don't you?" asked Michael. "We have had many battles with you over the centuries. You are no match for King Jesus, the eternal King of the universe. We are His faithful servants – Defenders of the Faith – and He has given us the strength and authority in Jesus' name to restrain you. Your evil cannot prevail for it is God Almighty who has resurrection power and He has redeemed the world!

Get back to your demonic strongholds buried in the earth's realm and stay away from the Lord's work, you miserable old wretch. You know Messiah Jesus is coming back soon and your days are numbered. Let us remind you of what the Lord Jesus, the Messiah of the world said to you long ago," admonished Gabriel.

The two specially anointed heavenly angels together, quoted Scripture out loud from Matthew 4:10: "Be gone, Satan! For it is written, 'YOU SHALL WORSHIP THE LORD YOUR GOD, AND SERVE HIM ONLY.'"

As soon as Michael and Gabriel quoted the Scripture from the book of Matthew, the devil in the form of the diabolical black wildcat vanished. The lights in the spacious room stopped flickering and the sizzling sounds that had taken over the computers stopped. Truly, the Word of God is more powerful than any two-edged sword and mighty in God for pulling down strongholds!

Exodus 23:20

"Behold, I am going to send an angel before you to guard you along the way, and to bring you into the place which I have prepared."

Chapter Eight

Moving Forward

Levi and Jesse tried to distract Yossi and his friends while Michael and Gabriel engaged in the spiritual battle with the devil. Then, without warning Michael and Gabriel walked into Fellowship Hall, both wearing big smiles.

"We don't think you will have any more trouble with your project," said Michael. "God has intervened and has taken care of the problem. We have tested all your equipment and it is running smoothly. We were able to recover all your lost data. You can get back to work as if nothing happened."

"What a relief," cried out Yossi. "I was really worried. I know I shouldn't worry because God is all-powerful and I do trust Him, but I am still human and I am still just a kid!"

"We understand," said Jesse. "It is human nature to worry. But you all have your faith and you can see how the Lord came through for all of you. Always remember Proverbs: 3:5-6:

'Trust in the Lord with all your heart, and lean not on your own understanding; in all your ways acknowledge Him, and He shall direct your paths.'"

"God's ways are not our ways, and when we place our trust in Him we can be sure He is working out things to our benefit," added Levi.

"Michael, Gabriel – would you like to stay and visit with us for a few days?" asked Jesse.

"We would love to stay and visit with all of you but we have another assignment that we must take care of right away. But we will try to come back again for another visit," replied Gabriel.

"Where is that you live?" asked Eli.

"Oh, well, it's kind of far from here, and we have to get going right away or we will be late for our next appointment. Eli, I am sure we will see all of you again, soon. When we have more time we will tell you all about ourselves. The most important thing to remember right now is to get this project completed for the Lord," said Michael.

"We know from our work that the devil and all his dark forces are setting traps all over this planet to trick as many people as possible into believing that there is no such place as hell and that Jesus – Yeshua is just another prophet or teacher. I think you guys have a great plan to thwart his nasty plans."

"Thank you for coming here so quickly and helping us," said Jesse.

"We are doing the Lord's work and are blessed to be in His service. We are more than happy to help," responded Michael.

"Those shirts you wear are really awesome," said Yossi. "Maybe when I grow up I'll have one like that, too. I like the logo on the shirt pockets: 'Defenders of the Faith.' I want to be a 'Defender of the Faith!'"

Gabriel spoke right up and said, "Well, it just happens that we have some extra shirts with us and he seemed to pull out of nowhere four white shirts with the golden logo on the front pockets."

"Wow!" said Yossi, as he rushed over to Gabriel. Peter, Jacob and Eli jumped right up from their chairs and they were each handed a shirt.

"Hey, this material feels really smooth, like silk, but it's strong too. I don't think I've ever felt anything like this before," said Eli. "And the gold logo is so vivid—definitely out of this world! Where did you get these incredible shirts?"

"I'll show you one day Eli," answered Michael. "The uniforms are created by God's decree! One day you will see the place where they make these shirts, one day soon," exclaimed Gabriel.

"But, we have to hurry up and get going *right now!*" said Michael. "Remember to use the Word of God as your weapon to ward off the enemy, and we *will* see all of you again!"

While the young boys were admiring their new shirts, Jesse and Levi pulled aside Michael and Gabriel.

"How bad was it over there?" asked Jesse.

"That old wretch, that old loser, Satan, nearly had the entire project derailed, but the Lord gave us super-strength from the power of His holy Word—His Scriptures," explained Michael. "He went from showing himself to be a fierce roaring wildcat but ended up wincing like a spineless alley cat spinning back into his demonically infested sphere, thanks to the Lord's intervention. We are Defenders of the Faith, but we cannot do anything without the Lord—without the power of Christ. In Him we are made strong!

We've had a lot of experience dealing with the devil and his deadly forces. This won't be the last time. We know, because in Revelation 12—in the Bible, the coming war in heaven is described. After that the devil will not be able to have access to heaven any more, and accuse believers of their weaknesses and wrong doings before the Father—when they fall into sin.

We know Jesus intercedes and defends those who are His because their sins are covered by His blood sacrifice. Every person falls short sometimes and falls into sin, even when they are trying to be obedient. The devil is going to get knocked down in that war and he will lose his access to heaven for good. And it won't be long now, considering how so many of the prophetic Scriptures are being fulfilled."

"Come on Michael," said Gabriel. "We really have to get going—right now."

Michael and Gabriel hurried out the front door of the building waving good-bye to everyone. Yossi ran after them to thank them again for their help and for the shirts. When he got outside there was no trace of Michael or Gabriel.

"They're gone," lamented Yossi with a confused look on his face. "How could they have left so fast? There is no trace of them at all. I don't see a car driving away and I can't hear their voices from a distance."

Levi immediately answered, "You know Yossi; some things are better left to our imagination. I am sure Michael and Gabriel are doing fine. They had another special job to work on. Let's get over to the game room at your house and get back to work."

Yossi walked with the rest of the guys over to his house, but he couldn't help but wonder how Michael and Gabriel were there one minute, and then gone the next.

"Those two guys were really something," said Jacob. "Did anyone notice that they looked kind of mature but didn't have any wrinkles or any gray hair? There is something really unusual about them. They were always so calm, like nothing could fluster them."

"Yeah," said Peter. "I hope we will see them again. I kind of get the feeling that they know a lot about a lot of things. And these shirts are ultra unique. We'll be the envy of everyone at school."

"All we have to think about right now is getting our work done," said Eli.

"You're right," said Yossi, but he continued to think out loud.

"You know, guys, Jesse and Levi kind of remind me of Michael and Gabriel. They all have super-bright, friendly eyes and look really healthy and fit. Did you see Gabriel lifting those heavy boxes in the sanctuary, as if they're as light as air? They sure seem to know a lot about God. They all have a sense of confidence, a radiance that makes them stand out from others. They seem to have a 'glow' about them. Maybe they take extra vitamins or something. I don't know. No, that can't be it. But there is something special and unusual about all four of those guys."

"Yossi, you are making some good observations," responded his pal, Jacob. "But right now we better finish up the last details of our project. We should have all our work completed by tomorrow night or by the next day for sure – if we keep plugging away. It has been so great working together like this."

"We can finish everything by tomorrow night," said Eli. "I hope everybody is as excited as I am about what we've been doing. Okay, that was a dumb thing to say. I *know* we are all excited. One more long night of work and we should have our project in perfect working order. Tomorrow we can check over the final details of our work and then we can get out into the world and reach lots of people. Now let's get in there and churn out some good stuff for God!"

Satan Will Be Cast Out of Heaven Forever

Satan will be permanently cast out of heaven during the Tribulation. Right now he roams the earth and goes back and forth between heaven and earth accusing the brethren before God the Father, and Jesus sits at the right hand of the Father acting as our a Advocate declaring all believers as righteous.

In a vision, the Lord Jesus Christ showed the apostle John a series of events that were to come in the last days. In the passage below, John describes what he saw regarding a future war in heaven. These events are recorded in Revelation 12:7-10, 12, the last book of the Bible:

> "And war broke out in heaven: Michael and his angels fought with the dragon [the devil]; and the dragon and his angels fought, but they did not prevail, nor was a place found for them in heaven any longer. So the great dragon was cast out, that serpent of old called the Devil and Satan, who deceives the whole world; he was cast to the earth, and his angels were cast with him.
>
> Then I heard a loud voice saying in heaven, 'Now salvation, and strength, and the kingdom of our God, and the power of His Christ have come, for the accuser of our brethren, who accused them before our God day and night, has been cast down. Therefore, rejoice O heavens, and you who dwell in them! Woe to the inhabitants of the earth, and the sea! For the devil has come down to you, having great wrath, because he knows that he has a short time.'"

We Are Made Righteous through Christ

Through salvation and faith in Jesus Christ we are made righteous because of His death sacrifice on the cross at Calvary.

> "If we confess our sins, He is faithful and righteous to forgive us our sins and to cleanse us from all unrighteousness.
>
> If we say that we have not sinned, we make Him a liar, and His word is not in us. My little children, I am writing these things to you that you may not sin.
>
> And if anyone sins, we have an Advocate with the Father, Jesus Christ the righteous; and He Himself is the propitiation for **our sins**; and not for ours only, but also for *those of* the whole world" (1 John 1:9-10; 2:1-2).

Once we are saved we are made righteous through faith in Messiah Jesus—apart from our performance. No matter how hard we try, not one of us can be without sin but through Christ we are forgiven and made righteous. When we do stumble and fall into sin, we should do just as we have read in the previous Scripture, "confess our sins" to the Advocate, "Jesus Christ the righteous." As born-again believers we are not without sin, but we are guiltless—forgiven, because of Christ's sacrifice on the cross and His gift of grace (unmerited favor), which He bestows on all those who belong to Him.

Chapter Nine

Back to Work

"**W**ow!" exclaimed Yossi. "My computer has never worked better than it is right now. Everything seems to be working better than ever."

"Let's get our software programs loaded up," said Eli. "We'll spend the next few hours checking through everything to make sure everything is integrated properly."

While Yossi and his friends worked on the finishing touches of their project, Jesse and Levi spent their time at Fellowship Hall working with Rachel, Zvi, Pastor Hezzie and the other volunteers.

"We have all the third-world countries covered with our many missionary friends. As far as the nations ruled by ruthless dictators, we have added some more undercover agents who will continue to smuggle in Bibles and help other believers spread the salvation message.

They also have contacts that have access to computers with good, strong printers that can print out the new tract we have created about the Rapture, the Tribulation and the Second Coming of Christ.

We'll email the tract as a PDF to our key undercover agents. It is miraculous how they're able to smuggle in so many Bibles," chuckled Levi. "Maybe some angels from heaven have something to do with it."

"Attention everyone!" announced Pastor Hezzie.

"I just received word from, Aaron in Tel Aviv, saying he has made contact with at least three-hundred ministries throughout the world who will be taking up the cost of supplying free Bibles to all those who wish to have them—once we start our campaign.

They will be available in any language. We also have about seven large Bible publishers willing to help these ministries by giving a huge discount for their publishing fees. What a miraculous blessing!

This is an unexpected turn of events. We are being blessed in ways I never imagined. Aaron told me that a couple of very friendly well-dressed gentlemen—Michael and Gabriel came to his ministry and offered their help in setting-up the free Bible distribution program.

Aaron had never met them before, but Michael and Gabriel told him that they had just been here, in Jerusalem, helping us. He said that the two visitors were able to get everyone they contacted to agree to help, and help very generously! What a couple of great friends Michael and Gabriel are."

Jesse and Levi smiled at each other. "Yes, they are very dedicated to the Lord and will go out of their way to help our project get underway," said Levi. "Who knows what else they will do to move our project along!"

"I would like to follow-up on some of the contacts we made earlier this week, and make sure that those folks understand how our program is going to work," added Jesse.

"It is always a good idea to double-check our work. Good communication is very important and sometimes even when we try our best, people can misunderstand each other. I will spend most of tomorrow morning contacting all the people on our list. I can send out some quick emails and some text messages to everyone, reminding them to be sure to carefully read over the information packets we sent."

"Great idea Jesse. You and Levi have been such a great help to us," said Pastor Hezzie.

"It has been our blessing, Pastor Hezzie. We are happy to be a part of such an important endeavor," remarked Levi.

"We are very glad to be working with you and Jesse. We feel like you are a part of our family," added Pastor Hezzi. "But it is getting late and we better call it a day. I think Yossi and his group will be joining us here tomorrow afternoon. Let's all get a good night's sleep and try to wrap up all the details tomorrow."

Jesse and Levi spent the rest of the evening in their rooms preparing for the next day's workload. Sleep was the last thing on their minds. They both prayed, quietly seeking the Lord's guidance so the final aspects of their mission would be a great success.

All their hard work was truly a joy as they saw things coming together. They both felt very comfortable with their new friends and were determined to do everything possible to make sure everyone involved in the project would receive a special blessing from God for all their dedication to further the gospel and warn others about the judgments that are soon to fall upon planet Earth.

Yossi and his pals didn't know it, but one of the young boys from their congregation frequently visited the Western Wall

to pray that all would go well with the campaign. He prayed
with great conviction and reverence to the Lord to help ensure
the worldwide success of the project. A mighty young prayer
warrior!

Our Shield of Protection

Ephesians 6:14-18

"Stand therefore, having girded your waist with truth, having put on the breastplate of righteousness, and having shod your feet with the preparation of the gospel of peace; above all, taking the shield of faith with which you will be able to quench all the fiery darts of the wicked one.

And take the helmet of salvation, and the sword of the Spirit, which is the word of God; praying always with all prayer and supplication in the Spirit, being watchful to this end with all perseverance and supplication for all the saints."

Chapter Ten

It's a Wrap!

"It looks like we have everything we need to get our message out to the world," said Eli. "We'll keep all our data and our ads right up-to-date every day. The participating churches and ministries around the world will have volunteers working 24/7 answering phones so when someone responds to the 'Free Gift' of salvation ad they will have a real person to talk to.

And now, thanks to the help we are getting from other ministries, everyone who wants a Bible will get one for free. Yossi, Peter, Jacob, are you organized on exactly how you will stay in touch with all our representatives?"

"We're organized Eli," replied Yossi. "We have everything ready to go. We'll always make sure things are running smoothly with our new software programs and mobile apps. We can also text messages to our representatives before we go to school in the morning and then after school too. We've divided up all our contacts into three groups. We will each be responsible for maintaining contact with one of the groups."

"And I will make sure all our ads are being placed properly onto all the top search engines, Web hosting sites and smartphones," said Eli. "We've worked hard to get everything running smoothly. And Peter, will you be sure to keep those flash ads up-to-date, especially for the smartphones so I can program them into our system?"

"No worries Eli," responded Peter. "I have developed several really catchy flash ads to get the attention of kids of all ages."

"Great. Okay guys, we better get over to Fellowship Hall to meet with Yossi's dad and the others," said Eli.

Yossi and his friends arrived at Fellowship Hall just as everyone else was arriving in the spacious, inviting room.

"Shalom everyone!" said Pastor Hezzie. "This is a very exciting day for us." He looked around the room to see that everyone was comfortably seated.

"We have all worked very hard to reach our goals. It appears that we are about ready to launch our campaign. First, Jesse and Levi will give us an update on what we have put together in our group. Then Yossi and his group will share what they have done."

"Yes, shalom everyone," said Jesse. "We are very grateful to have the privilege of being part of such a wonderful ministry. We have come up with one new Bible tract. At first we were working on several different tracts, but as a group, we made the decision that it would be best to place the salvation message, the Rapture and the Tribulation all in one tract – with our ministry logo and contact information on the back page. These Bible tracts can be downloaded on anyone's computer and printed out.

Yossi and his group have already created a way for the tract to be downloaded in any language by a simply clicking on the 'Choose Language' option link. We can also send the tract out as a PDF file or JPEG. We have created a template for the volunteers who would like to go to a printer and have them printed out in mass quantities. Those who wish to have templates in a particular language can quickly place an order with us and Pastor Hezzie can have it sent it out within forty-eight hours."

"Yes," said Levi. "We have already made hundreds of contacts throughout the world and we will be working closely with all of them. Our phones here will be ringing a lot, and our email inboxes will be loaded every day.

One of our great blessings is having the volunteers who will answer the phones at so many different ministries around the world. Our good friend, Aaron, in Tel Aviv has recruited dozens of believers to answer the phones at his ministry. He has a large building and can handle as many as two hundred people at a time.

Pastor Hezzie says he can handle about eighty people at a time to answer phones, here in his expanded office. We also have our friends who own large companies that send out advertisements in the form of mass mailings. They have definitely agreed to send out thousands of Bible tracts per bundle. Our contacts donating their printing presses will supply the tracts to them and then they will send out those tracts in mass mailings all over the world.

Jesse and I will be working closely with Pastor Hezzie, Zvi and Rachel and all our volunteers here in Jerusalem to make sure everything is running smoothly. One of the most important things we must remember is to stay in prayer throughout the day. Always keep in mind that we are fighting a spiritual battle. The Word of God is the most powerful weapon and prayer is very important to ward of the enemies of God."

"Thank you Jesse and Levi," said Pastor Hezzie. "Now let's hear from Yossi and his group."

Yossi stood up from his chair and walked to the front of the room.

"I think you all already have a good idea of what we have been working on. We are excited to say that the software programs we have developed are working very well, which will make it possible for us to reach millions of people worldwide. We have each taken on specific responsibilities to keep everything working properly," reported Yossi.

"We have all our representatives throughout the world ready to start their volunteers at the various ministries answering their phones. Between the volunteers and recruiters that we found, and the ones Jessie and Levi can count on—we have a lot of help.

As soon as someone clicks on the 'Free Gift' of salvation link with a smartphone, they will have the option of calling in to one of the phone numbers for more information.

All they will have to do is click on a designated link and their phone will automatically connect to a ministry in their area where a volunteer will pray with them or answer any questions about the Bible, salvation, the Rapture, the Tribulation or anything else related to the Scriptures.

All our volunteers have been told about the free Bibles that are available and they will offer them to anyone who wants one. The same goes for anyone who clicks on our ad on the Internet. All they will have to do is call the listed phone number, or click on our website link to view our information. And like Jesse said earlier, anyone can download a free tract from our website or through an email. Now Eli has a bit more to say about what we have ready to go."

Eli stood up and headed quickly toward Yossi, who was standing comfortably at the front of the meeting room.

"Shalom my friends!" exclaimed Eli. "I am confident that our campaign designed to reach multitudes for the Lord Jesus, is going to be a great success. Yossi, Jacob, Peter and I have concentrated mostly on all the technical details. First, I would like to show you the website we have created for our project."

Eli opened up his laptop computer and quickly accessed the new website.

"This is it!" Eli proudly proclaimed.

"Great color choices," said Rachel. "And the images are very appealing. I especially like the clouds and the rising sun in the background."

"As soon as we load the new tract, it will be right here on the first page," Eli continued. "Anyone who goes to this website will be able to download the tract, or share it with others through emails. Our contact information is easy to find, and we can always add new material to this site. After our meeting, why don't all of you take a closer look?

You may remember that earlier when we first started our campaign Yossi mentioned we would not leave out television. We also realize it is important to reach others through radio ads. Although we can reach a lot more people using our new software programs over the Internet and with our mobile apps, most people still do watch some television and listen to the radio. We have tried to come up with a new way to reach those folks, but using an advertising technique is probably the best approach. We have written an ad that should get anyone's attention. This is how it goes:

'Are you wondering why so many things in this world don't seem to make any sense? Why there is so much confusion and chaos everywhere? Are you worried about your future? Do you feel like something is not right with the life in general? Are you confused about world events and the dangerous uprisings and growing violence and loss of personal freedoms? We have the answer for you. It can be found in the greatest Book ever written. There is tremendous hope if only you would open your heart and mind to the One who loves you, no matter what.

We are living in the age of misinformation and deception, just the way the Scriptures said it would be in these last days. Yes, *these are* the last days. But there can be a very bright future for you. We can answer your questions if you would call this number right now. There is no fee involved, only a free uplifting message; a free gift that will save your life.'"

Yossi spoke up and said, "We will have a toll-free phone number or a local number posted at the end of the ad for each particular area. The ads will be written across the TV screen, but someone will also be speaking the words—a voiceover, especially for those who are blind or nearly blind and can't read a TV screen. Maybe Jesse and Levi can make a special graphic for the advertisement. The calls will go to one of the many ministries that we have recruited for our Internet and smartphone ads.

The same goes for the radio ads. There will be a call-in number. The many volunteers will share the salvation message over the phone and offer our free tracts and a free Bible. This is a more traditional approach which takes longer, but we don't think we can leave out reaching others through television or radio."

"We have compiled a list here for all of you, detailing what we have accomplished and how we will implement our technical programs so you can refer to it whenever you need to. Jacob has copies of the list that you can pick up from him after our meeting. Well, that's it for now," concluded Eli.

Pastor Hezzie stood up from his chair to casually say a few encouraging words and to close the meeting.

"Thank you Yossi, Eli, Peter, Jacob. We are all very proud of your hard work and efforts. We could not do any of this without all of your exceptional technical skills.

You are all very smart, and more important—very dedicated to the Messiah Jesus. The Lord has provided us with so many resources and hundreds of believers who are generously contributing to this cause," added Pastor Hezzie.

"I am still stunned and amazed at how much money has been donated by so many people to make this project possible. I think a great number of believers realize nothing is more important than doing the Lord's work – reaching others with the salvation message, alerting the lost to the Rapture, the Tribulation and the Lord's Second Coming. May He continue to bless our efforts as we get our campaign off the ground! Jesse and Levi, would you meet with Eli? Let's get that tract with our message loaded onto our great new website."

"Of course," responded Levi. "Jesse and I will meet with Eli and his group and work out the final details about when we can get our campaign started full force. We'll also make a graphic for the TV ads and get that to the boys as soon as possible. I expect we should be able to get all the advertising secured onto the various television and radio stations within a week, thanks to our many volunteers.

"We have so many people willing to help in every city throughout the world! Jesse and I will be in charge of that, as well as the mass mailings. Jesse will also be working every day with his undercover contacts located in all the dangerous nations that are ruled by dictators. We have some fantastic, brave believers on alert and ready to get started. And we are in very close contact with our missionary friends located in the third world nations as well."

Eli added, "We should have all our contacts ready to go forward very soon. We'll follow through the rest of this week and we should have all the details in place and ready to go by the weekend."

"Good enough! We'll consider next Monday our official day to launch our campaign," replied Pastor Hezzie.

As the meeting ended there was the exciting sound of chattering, happy voices echoing throughout the room. Zvi approached Jesse and Levi.

"We could not have done so much so fast without the two of you," he said.

"Are you kidding?" responded Jesse. "We could not have done any of this without the help of all of you.

And your little brother and his friends are so talented. Those kids are amazing. The truth is, without their technical and creative talents we would not be anywhere near ready to reach millions."

"You are right about that," said Zvi. "It is as if God has given every one of the kids in Yossi's group a special anointing to move this project forward."

"We have an awesome God, and we give all the glory and praise to Him for bringing us all together," added Levi.

"Yes, to God be the glory," said Jesse. "I think it is great how Yossi and his friends all get along so well with one other. They understand that working together as a team will bring success to our project. They are unusually mature and responsible. Have you noticed how they respect each other? They know how to work hard and have fun at the same time.

I overheard Peter tell Eli that he would like to have special youth group events on Friday nights at Fellowship Hall. Jacob's brother is the lead singer in a great worship band and they are willing to be the entertainment every week. The teens can hang out together and work on reaching others for Christ at the same time."

"That sounds like a great idea," said Zvi. "No doubt, they will have the place packed in no time. Every kid in Jerusalem will want to come, if Yossi and Eli have anything to do with it. They are very popular."

Just as Zvi, Levi and Jesse were finishing up their conversation, pastor Hezzie yelled out:

"Hold on everyone! One more thing: Let's all meet in the sanctuary next Sunday evening for prayer and we will officially start our campaign on Monday morning."

"We'll be there!" yelled out everyone in the room with enormous excitement. "We'll be there!"

Eagerly Waiting for Messiah Jesus

Paul the apostle wrote these awesome words:

"Looking for that blessed hope, and the glorious appearing of the great God and our Savior Jesus Christ; who gave himself for us, that he might redeem us from all iniquity and purify unto himself a peculiar people zealous of good works" (Titus 2:13-14).

Finally, there is laid up for me the crown of righteousness, which the Lord, the righteous Judge, will give to me on that day, and not to me only but also to all those who have loved His appearing" (2 Timothy 4:8).

Chapter Eleven

Five, Four, Three, Two, One the Campaign Begins!

Sunday evening arrived quickly. Pastor Hezzie led the group in prayer: "Heavenly Father, our Father, we come before you this evening to ask for your mighty blessing. We are so grateful to be part of this outpouring of your love to bring others into your Kingdom. We ask that you would keep all obstacles away and open all the doors that need to be opened so we can act as your faithful and mighty ambassadors. Thank you for making it possible to move us forward so quickly. Please give each one of us wisdom as we get our campaign out into the world. We give you all the glory and praise. We ask this in the eternal name of Jesus. Amen."

And everyone said, "Amen!"

Pastor Hezzie continued to address the group: "It is wonderful to be here together with all of you. I understand everything is all set and ready to go. I want to thank all of you for your dedication and hard work. These past two weeks have gone by so quickly. It seems like we just *started* talking about our outreach project, and here we are now ready to launch our campaign. Is there anyone that would like to share anything?"

"Yes, I would like to," responded Yossi, waving his left hand up in the air.

"When I started my spring vacation a couple of weeks ago, I had no idea what the Lord had planned for me. This has been the best vacation of my life. I am so excited to be heading back to school knowing that we have accomplished so much.

I want to reassure everyone here that Eli, Peter, Jacob and I will be monitoring our work every moment we can. We have developed a great communication system. All four of us are thrilled to be working together. We promise we will keep our attention focused on winning those lost souls."

"Thank you Yossi," said Pastor Hezzie.

Levi stood up and gave his update.

"Our team members have worked very hard over at Fellowship Hall. We are ready — everything is in order just as planned. We have communicated with our contacts everywhere and are very confident each person involved is one-hundred-percent committed to the cause of Christ and will follow through on the work ahead. After tomorrow, Jesse and I will be traveling around the world to personally meet with our various contacts.

We have discussed this with Pastor Hezzie and he will stay in close contact with us. After our meetings, we will be taking a sabbatical and it will not be possible to reach us. But, please know that we will be with all of you in prayer."

Jesse stood up and added:

"We are so blessed to have met all of you. One of the best parts of spending time together is the comfort of knowing for sure that we have all of eternity to be together, that our good-byes are only temporary. Once we begin our sabbatical, we will be praying and many others we know will be praying with us to ensure the success of the campaign. You have all worked very hard. We are sure you have grace and favor from the Lord. Rest assured in the Lord's shalom (peace) knowing the future is going to be spectacular for all of us.

We look forward to the day we are all together and with our Yeshua, forever. Levi and I will try to check in with you in the future, but we don't know specifically what the Lord has planned for us. We are so thankful for the hospitality we have been given here in Jerusalem. We will always remember all the delicious meals that Sarah prepared for us. May the Lord have a special ministry for her in heaven feeding hungry angels and saints!

And Yossi, you and the guys are the greatest. Every kid in the world should be like you, Eli, Jacob and Peter. What love and devotion you have for the Lord. Rachel and Zvi—Levi and I both think of you as close family. You brought us here to work on this project. We love you!

Pastor Hezzie and Sarah, we respect and love you so very much. And to all our volunteers here in this room, in no way could we have accomplished this much without you. We love all of you, too. May the Lord bless each and every one of you as each day ushers us toward the climax of earth's history and the Lord's return.

Keep your hearts and thoughts focused on Him, the King of kings, the Lord of lords, our awesome King and Savior, Yeshua Ha Mashiach. Trust Him no matter what and continue to make Him the center of your lives. And one day soon, you will hear His shout at the last trump and you will be on your way up to meet Him in the air, and be forever with Him in glory!"

Yossi and Eli were taken aback to hear the unexpected news that Jesse and Levi would be leaving Jerusalem so soon.

There seemed to be a quiet urgency related to Levi and Jesse's departure.

"I'm really going to miss Jesse and Levi," whispered Yossi to Eli. "The way they talk it sounds like we might not see them again."

"No, Yossi!" replied Eli. "They said we would all be together again."

"But I think they were trying to give us a hint that it might not be until *after* we are all taken up in the Rapture," said Yossi. "Where do you think they are going on their sabbatical?"

"I don't know," replied Eli. "Let's say good-bye to them right now. We have to get home and get ourselves together for school tomorrow."

Yossi and Eli hurried over to Jesse and Levi.

"Hey you two, we are really going to miss you," said Jesse.

"We're going to miss both of you, too!" exclaimed Yossi. "May we call you sometime or come visit you?"

"You can call us before we take our sabbatical, but after that it won't be possible to reach us," responded Levi.

"Well, can you get in touch with us after your sabbatical?" asked Eli.

"Eli, Yossi, sometimes the Lord does things that we don't understand. But we promise you both, you *will* see Levi and me again and it won't be long. Now, we are counting on you guys to carry on for us. We sure will miss you a lot. Remember, we will be praying for each of you, and before you know it we will all be together again."

Jesse and Levi hugged Eli and Yossi. Peter and Jacob came over and joined in with the hugs.

"We better go," said Eli.

"Okay," responded Yossi. "We'll walk with you," said Peter and Jacob.

While the four boys were walking over to Yossi's house, Yossi said, "You know, I want to check something in my Bible."

As soon as they got inside the house, Yossi ran upstairs to his room and looked up Revelation 12:7 in his Bible. Then he looked up Jude 1:9. Then he looked up several verses in Luke 1.

"Hmmm, just as I thought," Yossi said to himself: "The archangel Michael and the angel Gabriel. No, it can't be. But then again, the Michael and Gabriel that were here sure were unusual. And what about the way they seemed to disappear when they left?"

"Eli, Peter and Jacob – come on up here, you guys," called out Yossi.

The three boys were upstairs in no time! Yossi placed his Bible in front of them.

"Look, look at these Scriptures." Yossi pointed at the Scriptures and flipped the pages as he read aloud.

"They are all about the archangel Michael and the angel Gabriel – here, in Revelation 12:7, Jude 1:9, and a few more in Luke, chapter one. And look right here – it says right here in Genesis 28:12 and in John 1:51, that angels can visit earth from heaven!"

Eli looked at Yossi.

"Oh, come on buddy. Michael and Gabriel can't be the same, well, you know, they *really* are unusual. But it's not possible!" asserted Eli.

"Anything is possible with God," added Peter.

"Peter is right," said Jacob. Maybe Michael and Gabriel *are* angels. And how about the way they whipped out those four shirts from nowhere? I mean – those two are *really* something. And they sure got the demonic strongholds off our project, fast!"

"Come on, you guys!" exclaimed Eli. "Am I the *only* one in this bunch that is not delusional? I think you all ate *way* too much pizza for dinner tonight and you are all imagining things—like you would in a silly dream after eating too much junk food!

I think we should all just calm down and not read anything into any of this. Let's call it a day and get some rest. Everything will be clearer to us once we get some good sleep. I think all three of you are imaging things and should slow down a bit."

Just as Eli finished his speech, the doorbell rang. Sarah yelled upstairs to the boys:

"Yossi! Everyone! Come down here please."

The four boys charged down the stairs to find out what Yossi's mom wanted.

"Look!" said Sarah, "A special delivery package for all of you – for Yossi, Eli, Peter and Jacob. Your names are all written in beautiful bold gold letters on the lid. What a beautiful white box!"

"Wow. The box looks really sturdy and there is something special about it but I can't quite figure out what. Who is it from?" Yossi asked.

"Let's open it and find out," said Jacob. "You open it Yossi. Hurry up!"

Yossi carefully opened the sealed package. When he lifted the lid off the box and looked inside – a huge smile came to his face.

"Look. It's four more shirts with the 'Defenders of the Faith' logo on the shirt pocket!"

"Is there a card inside? Who is it from?" asked Peter.

"No, there is no card," replied Yossi.

"Mom, which delivery carrier left the package?" asked Yossi.

"I don't know, Yossi. The doorbell rang, and when I looked out the window and opened the door, the package was sitting on the welcome mat. I did notice in the dark that the package seemed to have a 'glow' to it. But I didn't see the delivery truck," answered Sarah.

"Well," said Eli. "We better get all our stuff together. I still have to drive Jacob and Peter home. We all have school tomorrow and plenty to do to make sure the first day of our campaign is running smoothly."

"Okay," answered the other three boys.

They all headed back upstairs to Yossi's room. Peter carefully carried the white box. Yossi immediately shut the door once they were all inside his room.

"Can you *believe* this? It has to be some sort of message – a sign," pleaded Yossi.

"What do you mean?" asked Eli. "Oh come on, you don't think those shirts came from...? No, it's not possible. Someone is probably playing a game with us."

"It's a sign! The package is from Michael and Gabriel. Those shirts *cannot* be from anyone else. I think God is trying to tell us we are on the right track about figuring out that Michael and Gabriel came here from heaven on a special mission to help us," insisted Yossi.

No one said even one word after Yossi made his declaration. It was very quiet in the room for a few minutes.

"Okay. I will admit that the situation with the package is really weird," said Eli. "But, come on – angels from heaven sending us shirts?"

"Yep, I am convinced," declared Yossi.

"Well, we can talk about it tomorrow. Right now we better get going," exclaimed Eli. "Come on Peter, Jacob. We all have to get home."

"Okay then," said Jacob.

The three boys quietly walked down the stairway and then outside and into Eli's car. Just as Eli was about to start the ignition, the boys saw Jesse and Levi walking directly toward them waving their hands, trying to get the attention of the three young men. Eli rolled down his car window.

"Hey guys," We are really going miss you," said Levi, as he placed his left hand on the side of the car's window ledge. "Now remember the most important thing is to love the Lord, and keep studying His Scriptures. We promise everything is going to go great with this campaign."

As Peter listened, he noticed a very unusual gold ring on Levi's finger.

"We just wanted to say goodbye again. Now, be sure to drive carefully."

As Levi lifted up his hand to wave good-bye, Jacob noticed that on top of the ring in small letters were written the words: Defenders of the Faith. He quickly looked at Jesse's hands to see if he had a ring too – and he did. It looked like the exact same kind of ring Levi was wearing.

"Hey," said Jacob. "Those rings are really cool! I have never seen rings that look so gold. And what about the inscription?" asked Peter.

Levi took off his ring and handed the ring to Peter and said, "You mean this – Defenders of the Faith?"

"Yes, that *is* what I mean," replied Peter.

Jesse took off his ring and gave it to Jacob. And then he looked at Eli and said: "We just happen to have two more rings; one for you Eli and the other one is for Yossi."

"Unreal," exclaimed Eli. "This is the most incredible ring! What kind of gold is this? This is the richest looking gold I have ever seen. Check it out guys. Look at this awesome raised gold lettering on top. Each letter is so perfectly inscribed. I'll text Yossi and tell him to come right down here."

A few minutes later, Yossi was standing by the car next to Jesse and Levi. Jesse handed a ring to Yossi.

"Way cool," said Yossi. "Is this for me? I have never seen anything like this before. A 'Defenders of the Faith' ring! I will always wear it!"

"Okay guys, we better get going back to Fellowship Hall to finish up a few things," said Levi.

"Just remember, keep your focus on the Lord, study your Bibles every day and always remember that the Word of God is the most powerful weapon, and *always* be 'Defenders of the Faith.' We have to go, but we *will* see you all again, soon!"

As Jesse and Levi walked toward Fellowship Hall, Yossi opened the passenger door of Eli's car, got inside and climbed into the back seat.

"I think Jesse and Levi are connected to Michael and Gabriel," said Yossi. "What I mean is that I think that all four of them are messengers from God. The Bible teaches about 'entertaining angels unaware' in Hebrews 13:2. First we get the shirts from Michael and Gabriel, and now these awesome rings."

"And how about the way Rachel and Zvi spotted Jesse and Levi on the sidewalk the day after she had the dream about the Rapture?" asked Jacob.

"Rachel told me that all of a sudden Jesse and Levi were standing on the sidewalk on the street where she had been walking, and that they seemed to appear out of nowhere. And now Jesse and Levi are telling us that we won't be able to contact them on their 'sabbatical.' It sounds like they might be going back to heaven, if that is where they are really from."

"Oh, come on Yossi, Jacob," said Eli. "It is really getting *way too late* for all of this. I think we all need a good night's sleep so we can think clearly. Our imaginations are on overdrive right now. It is my car that should be in overdrive as I drive home to get some sleep! Yossi, you better get upstairs and into bed. We'll see you in the morning. I'll drive Peter and Jacob home and then I will hit the sack."

As soon as Yossi got back upstairs to his bedroom, he steadily peered out his window taking in all the stars and the glistening bright-golden moonlight. After much thinking and silent heart-felt worship unto the Lord, he prayed:

"My Father in heaven – I want to say, I think I understand why Jesse and Levi came here – and also Michael and Gabriel. If they did come from heaven to help us, then you must be coming back very soon. I will do my best to be a Defender of the Faith.

I want to do nothing more than serve you. You are my great hero, and I can't wait to see you. Please show Eli the truth. I think Peter and Jacob, get it, I think they agree that Jesse, Levi, Michael and Gabriel all came here from heaven on a mission."

Just as Yossi was finishing up his prayer, his phone rang. It was Eli.

"Hey, Yossi, I just dropped off Peter and Jacob. I'm parked near the Old City – just thinking. You might be right. I mean about the angel thing. I was thinking about everything that has happened over the past couple of weeks.

Everything has been so surreal. Do you know what I mean? Did you catch that little bit at the meeting tonight when Jesse was raving about your mom's cooking and how he hoped that the Lord would have a special ministry for her in heaven 'to feed hungry *angels* and saints?' When he said that I did get a strong, funny feeling that he was wishing that for himself!

And he always has that innocent, but mischievous look on his face, like he knows something other people don't.

And I have been admiring the ring Jesse gave me. I was looking at it, and on its underside I discovered that there are some more letters in Hebrew. Are you wearing your ring?" asked Eli.

"Yes, I am," replied Yossi. I think it is the coolest most awesome ring I have ever seen."

"Well, take it off and look on the underside."

Yossi took off his ring and sure enough on the underside of the ring were written some Hebrew letters. When translated into English, the letters read: **King of Kings and Lord of Lords.**

Also included was a Scripture reference pointing to the Rapture: Thessalonians 4:16-18.

"Look, it's another message Eli, it's another message! He is coming soon. It's a Rapture message!"

"I think you are right, Yossi," replied Eli. "I had to think about everything that has happened since we met Jesse and Levi, and I can't deny that they are both very unusual. And it is obvious that their friends, Michael and Gabriel are amazing. I think they had to go back to heaven. The Lord must have called them back for some reason.

So it is up to *us* now, to be Defenders of the Faith as we get our campaign off the ground. I'll call Peter and Jacob. They are both convinced that the Lord sent His holy angels to help accelerate our campaign. We won't say anything to anyone else about this – for now anyway.

The four of us have to stick together and stand in the front-lines of this spiritual war as Defenders of the Faith. And before we know it, we will all be standing face to face with our wonderful Savior, our Messiah – when He calls us home in the Rapture. But in the meantime, we have a very important job to do. We don't have any time to waste!"

"I'm ready Eli," said Yossi. "I am very excited about our campaign. To God be, all the glory, forever and ever. I am convinced that Jesse, Levi, Michael and Gabriel came here from heaven to help us.

I wonder if they can see what we are doing, from up there? God is a God of wonder. I don't understand many things about Him, but I have great faith and I know He is real. His Holy Scriptures and prayer are our direct lifelines to Him. So many prophecies have already been fulfilled. Jesus *is* our Messiah and I can't wait to see Him in Person one day soon!"

"Me too, buddy, we serve an awesome God. But we better get some sleep, Yossi," replied Eli. "It's getting very late."

"You're right Eli. Good night. And thanks for calling. Now I can sleep in peace knowing that my best friend believes what I was saying about being visited by God's holy angels."

Yossi clicked off his phone and stood quietly for a few minutes by his window, peacefully gazing out at the whimsical sparkling-golden stars anchored throughout the vast mysterious dark-blue, clear night sky. All of a sudden, he saw a group of stars shoot across the sky. They seemed to spell out:

"Surely, I am coming quickly!"

The End

Part Two

Jesus Wants You to Spend Eternity with Him

God's Promise to the Faithful

1 Corinthians 2:9-10

"But as it is written: Eye has not seen, nor ear heard. Nor have entered into the heart of man the things, which God has prepared for those who love Him. But God has revealed them to us through His Spirit. For the Spirit searches all things, yes, the deep things of God."

Chapter Twelve

The Rapture—Snatching Away—Of All True Believers

"Behold, I tell you a mystery: We shall not all sleep [die], but we shall all be changed—in a moment, in the twinkling of an eye, at the last trumpet, For the trumpet will sound, and the dead will be raised incorruptible, and we shall be changed" (1 Corinthians 15:51-52).

"For the Lord Himself will descend from heaven with a shout, with the voice of an archangel, and with the trumpet of God. And the dead in Christ will rise first. Then we who are alive and remain shall be caught up [Rapture] together with them in the clouds to meet the Lord in the air. And thus we shall always be with the Lord. Therefore comfort one another with these words" (1 Thessalonians 4:16-18).

The Lord Jesus Christ promises that all true believers will receive a new body, just like His. A body that is tangible but that also transcends matter. Beam me up, Jesus!

"Beloved, now we are children; and it has not yet been revealed, we shall be like Him, for we shall see Him as He is" (1 John 3:2).

"For our citizenship is in heaven, from which we also eagerly wait for the Savior, the Lord Jesus Christ, who will transform our lowly body that it may be conformed to His glorious body, according to the working by which He is able even to subdue all things to Himself" (Philippians 3:20).

The Tribulation as Forewarned by Jesus the Messiah

"For then there will be great tribulation, such as has not been since the beginning of the world until this time, no, nor ever shall be" (Matthew 24:21).

"While they are saying, 'Peace and safety!' like birth pangs upon a woman with child; and they [unbelievers] shall not escape" (1 Thessalonians 5:3).

The Tribulation will last seven years. Those years will be the last seven years of world history, as we know it. At the end of the Tribulation the Lord Jesus will return. He will renew the earth and will be in charge of the entire world. Planet Earth will be a rejuvenated, beautiful and blessed place. Jesus will reign and rule from Jerusalem.

It will begin very suddenly. All those who have placed their faith in Christ—all born-again believers, will have been already taken up to the safety of heaven in the Rapture, and will not go through the Tribulation. All those who are *not* true born-again believers will be left on earth to suffer greatly under the dictatorship of the Antichrist. Those days will be the most horrific days in world history, especially the last three and one-half years.

"The Lord is not slow about His promise, as some count slowness, but is patient toward you, not wishing for any to perish but for all to come to repentance" (2 Peter 3:9).

"For whosoever shall call upon the name of the Lord shall be saved" (Romans 10:13).

Don't Worry about the
Tribulation if You Are Saved

If you are saved you will be taken-up in the Rapture *before* the Tribulation begins. If not, you will be left behind to suffer the most horrific time in world history.

"Let not your heart be troubled; you believe in God, believe also in Me. In My Father's house are many mansions; if it were not so, I would have told you. I go to prepare a place for you. And if I go and prepare a place for you, I will come again and receive you to Myself; that where I am, there you may be also" (John 14:1-3).

Choose Heavenly Wisdom

James 3:13-18

"Who among you is wise and understanding? Let him show by his good behavior his deeds in the gentleness of wisdom.

But if you have bitter jealousy and selfish ambition in your heart, do not be arrogant and *so* lie against the truth. This wisdom is not that which comes down from above, but is earthly, natural, demonic.

For where jealousy and selfish ambition exist, there is disorder and every evil thing. But the wisdom from above is first pure, then peaceable, gentle, reasonable, full of mercy and good fruits, unwavering, without hypocrisy.

And the seed whose fruit is righteousness is sown in peace by those who make peace."

Beware of Wolves in Sheep's Clothing

Jesus warned in the last days as the Tribulation years draw near, corrupt Bible teachers, pastors and professing Christians (with wrong heart motives and hidden agendas) will infiltrate churches and ministries for selfish gain, adulation and fame claiming they are doing "work" for the Lord. (And some of them believe they really are!) Many will teach confusing unbiblical messages and doctrines. They will fool and mislead vast numbers of people but those with discerning spirits will eventually catch-on to the shady personas of these deceivers. These imposters can never fool God. The good men and women of God who are truly serving Him are very valuable and need to be encouraged.

Humility is the mark of wisdom, so is a sincere godly, loving spirit and a contrite heart (not fake humility). Beware of those who claim to be Christians but treat others rudely with prideful, superior attitudes. God is not mocked and those individuals will have to answer to the Lord one day and suffer the consequences of their shameful behavior. Those who are genuinely walking with the Lord will treat others with sincerity, respect and kindness— never falsely accusing others or reading untruths into situations. "Whoever sows injustice reaps calamity, and the rod they wield in fury will be broken" (Proverbs 22:8 NIV).

Please don't let the rude behavior of some who call themselves Christians keep you from coming to faith and salvation in Christ. As long as we live in this fallen world there will always be individuals who will use the name of God inappropriately as a means to a selfish end. Always stay focused on the greatness of Jesus (not the behavior of self-serving people). Choose your friends wisely and don't form your opinion about God based on the shallow character of inauthentic Christians. If someone claims to be walking with God but shows signs of hypocrisy, insincerity, disrespect and worldly compromise, be careful.

For example, you know someone is spiritually and morally corrupt when he or she defends and exclaims that an obviously guilty person caught lying and cheating has integrity, and instead deliberately, unjustly and irrationally blames and condemns an innocent person—by distorting their good intentions and twisting the facts. "Woe to those who call evil good, and good evil; who put darkness for light, and light for darkness; who put bitter for sweet, and sweet for bitter!" (Isaiah 5:20).

"For such are false apostles, deceitful workers, transforming themselves into apostles of Christ. And no wonder! For Satan himself transforms himself into an angel of light. Therefore it is no great thing if his ministers also transform themselves into ministers of righteousness, whose end will be according to their works" (2 Corinthians 11:13-15).

"But know this, that in the last days perilous times will come: For men will be lovers of themselves, lovers of money, boasters, proud, blasphemers, disobedient to parents, unthankful, unholy, unloving, unforgiving, slanderers, without self-control, brutal, despisers of good, traitors, headstrong, haughty, lovers of pleasure rather than lovers of God, having a form of godliness but denying its power. And from such people turn away!" (1 Timothy 3:1-5)

The Bible is filled with admonitions for holy living and also warnings to those who mock God by gossiping, slandering, maliciously and deliberately scheming and plotting against others with the intention of causing them harm. Deceptive underhanded behavior is an abomination to the Lord. A person who travels in Christian circles praising the name of the Lord but is involved in atrocious deeds in private is a very disturbed individual, void of a relationship with the true and living God.

Pay attention to the words a person uses. If his or her way of speaking is often crass or filled with negativity and judgment toward others, beware. "A perverse person stirs up conflict, and a gossip separates close friends" (Proverbs 16:28 NIV).

Many trustworthy Christians who love the Lord can be found but if a person professes faith in Jesus Christ but lives like a rebellious hypocrite, do not keep company with that person. He or she is in great need of deliverance and repentance. A more productive way to spend time for such people would to be to get right with the Lord, truly repent and become faithful disciples leading others to Christ.

"Whoever secretly slanders his neighbor, him I will destroy; the one who has a haughty look and a proud heart, him I will not endure" (Psalm 101:5).

"These six *things* the Lord hates, yes, seven *are* an abomination to Him: A proud look, A lying tongue, hands that shed innocent blood, a heart that devises wicked plans, feet that are swift in running to evil, a false witness *who* speaks lies, And one who sows discord among brethren" (Proverbs 6:16-19).

In the very famous fairy tale, *Cinderella*, Cinderella's evil stepmother was extremely jealous of her beauty and charm. So were her two wicked and uncomely stepsisters. They hated the lovely Cinderella and obsessively schemed against her. (She was no fool and she knew!) But in the end, Cinderella was rescued by Prince Charming. So it is in real life for women of all ages—who are mistreated and viciously slandered by devious, mean-spirited jealous people.

Jesus is the Prince—the King, and He rescues and protects His righteous and judges the wicked. These same dynamics of jealousy and mistreatment also occur against boys, young men and grown men. Jealousy, hatred and anger are very destructive emotions. But be of good cheer, God always faithfully protects those who belong to Him.

"For nothing is secret that will not be revealed, nor anything hidden that will not be known and come to light" (Luke 8:17).

"Though his hatred is covered by deceit, his wickedness will be revealed before the assembly. Whoever digs a pit will fall into it, and he who rolls a stone will have it roll back on him" (Proverbs 26:26-27).

Three Key End-Time Players:

Antichrist, the False Prophet and Satan

Antichrist Will Control the World

In the Bible the Antichrist is called "the man of sin, the son of perdition." He is also called the "prince who is to come" who shall confirm a covenant with "the many" which is always expressly in reference to Israel in all the relevant verses in the book of Daniel (verses 11:33, 39; 9:27; 12:3).

The Antichrist will be a very deceptive man who will rule the entire world throughout the Tribulation years. He will fool many people into thinking he is a great leader and that he can solve all the problems in the world. But he will prove to be the most evil person who has ever lived. He will make it impossible to live in the world without becoming a slave to his rules.

The Great Tribulation is in reference to the halfway point of the seven-year Tribulation when the Antichrist will be literally indwelt by Satan, himself. He and his cohorts will be in control, severe persecutions will abound. No one will be able to function in the world system without taking the "mark of the beast."

Revelation 13:16

"He causes all both small and great, rich and poor, free and slave, to receive a mark on their right hand or on their foreheads, and that no one may buy or sell except one who has the mark of the beast, or the number of his name [666]."

Revelation 14:9-11

"Then a third angel followed them, saying with a loud voice, 'If anyone worships the beast and his image, and receives *his* mark on his forehead or on his hand, he himself shall also drink of the wine of the wrath of God, which is poured out full strength into the cup of His indignation.

He shall be tormented with fire and brimstone in the presence of the holy angels and in the presence of the Lamb.' And the smoke of their torment ascends forever and ever and they have no rest day or night, who worship the beast and his image, and whoever receives the mark of his name."

The False Prophet

The False Prophet will be the wicked religious leader who works closely with the Antichrist during the Tribulation. He will lead the world church (the apostate one-world religion) working to keep people in submission to the Antichrist's dastardly agenda.

"Then the beast [Antichrist] was captured, and with him the false prophet who worked signs in his presence, by which he deceived those who received the mark of the beast and those who worshiped his image. These two were cast alive into the lake of fire burning with brimstone" (Revelation 19:20).

The Unholy Trinity

The unholy trinity is always in reference to the Antichrist, the False Prophet and Satan himself.

Chapter Thirteen

The Second Coming of Jesus Christ

Matthew 24:29-31

"Immediately after the tribulation of those days the sun will be darkened, and the moon will not give its light; the stars will fall from heaven, and the powers of the heavens will be shaken.

Then the Son of Man [Jesus Christ] will appear in heaven and all the tribes of the earth will mourn, and they will see the Son of Man coming on the clouds of heaven with power and glory."

When Jesus returns bodily and visibly at the Second Coming, at the end of the Tribulation, He does not come alone. He brings His saints with Him. Who are these saints? Every Christian is called a saint because we are saved by grace and given the gift of righteousness through Christ. All believers taken-up in the Rapture before the Tribulation will be part of Christ's "armies of heaven clothed in fine white linen" following Him on white horses. He comes to make judgments, put an end to the rule of the Antichrist and set-up His literal 1000-year millennial reign on the rejuvenated earth.

Jesus returns to earth as a great warrior. He will judge the people and the nations and level the socio-economic ills of the world, and rule the earth:

"In His days the righteous shall flourish, and abundance of peace, until the moon is no more. He shall have dominion also from sea to sea, and from the River to the ends of the earth. Yes, all kings shall fall down before Him; all nations shall serve Him" (Psalm 72:7-8, 11).

The Lord's Mighty Return

Revelation 19:11-16

"Now I [John the apostle] saw heaven opened, and behold, a white horse. And He who sat on him *was* called Faithful and True, and in righteousness He judges and makes war. His eyes *were* like a flame of fire, and on His head *were* many crowns.

He had a name written that no one knew except Himself. He *was* clothed with a robe dipped in blood, and His name is called The Word of God. And the armies in heaven, clothed in fine linen, white and clean, followed Him on white horses.

Now out of His mouth goes a sharp sword, that with it He should strike the nations. And He Himself will rule them with a rod of iron. He Himself treads the winepress of the fierceness and wrath of Almighty God. And He has on *His* robe and on His thigh a name written: KING OF KINGS AND LORD OF LORDS."

Jude and Zechariah both wrote how the Lord will return to with His saints:

"Now Enoch, the seventh from Adam, prophesied about these men also saying, "Behold the Lord comes with ten thousands of His saints. Thus the LORD my God will come and all the saints with You.

Then the LORD will go forth and fight against those nations, as He fights in the day of battle. And in that day His feet will stand on the Mount of Olives, which faces Jerusalem on the east.

And the Mount of Olives shall be split in two from east to west; making a very large valley; half of the mountain shall move toward the north and half of it toward the south" (Jude 1:14; Zechariah 14:5b; 14:3-4).

The prophet, Zechariah's revelation that the Messiah of Israel will rule and reign on earth:

"Sing and rejoice, O daughter of Zion! For behold, I am coming and I will dwell in your midst," says the LORD. Many nations will be joined to the LORD in that day, and they shall become My people. And I will dwell with them in your midst. Then you will know that the LORD of hosts has sent Me to you. And the LORD will take possession of Judah and His inheritance in the Holy Land and will again choose Jerusalem" (Zechariah 2:10-12).

Daniel, the prophet also envisioned the future event of Christ's Second Coming and the start of the Messiah's reign on earth:

"I was watching in the night visions, and behold, One like the Son of Man, Coming with the clouds of heaven! He came to the Ancient of Days [God in Aramaic], and they brought Him near before Him.

Then to Him was given glory and a kingdom that all peoples, nations, and languages should serve Him. His dominion is an everlasting dominion, which shall not pass away, and His kingdom the one which shall not be destroyed" (Daniel 7:13-15).

The Millennial Reign of Messiah Jesus

The Millennium is a period of time beginning immediately after the Second Coming of Christ, and will continue for a period of one-thousand-years.

"And the LORD shall be King over all the earth. In that day it shall be—"The LORD *is* one," And His name one." —Zechariah 14:9

After the Millennium, the eternal kingdom will begin, as referenced in Revelation 21 and 22. But first, all born-again believers will taken-up to heaven in the Rapture while the Tribulation takes place on earth. In Revelation 20:4-6, John wrote that Messiah Jesus is going to be literally, physically ruling upon the earth during the one- thousand-year millennium. All true believers in their new, immortal glorified bodies will be assisting Him.

Messiah Jesus will return at the end of the Tribulation, reestablish the earth and the heavens, set-up His millennial kingdom, and sit upon the throne of His glory, the throne of David. His righteous order will be implemented. Israel will be leveled at the beginning of the Millennium (Isaiah 40:4), and Mount Zion will be a high mountain (Isaiah 2:2). The millennial city of Jerusalem will be at the top of Mount Zion. Messiah Jesus will continue to cleanse from sin those who receive Him during the Millennium.

Those who survive the Tribulation, the burning fire of the earth, and do who not take the mark of the beast and get saved at the end of the Tribulation will enter the Millennium in their natural bodies. Some will not get the gospel in its fullness until they actually see the Lord. All believers in their new glorified bodies, those who were taken-up in the Rapture will be given responsibilities according to their faithful service and devotion to the Lord, as recorded in: Luke 19:11-27; Revelation 20:2-6; Revelation 2:26-28; 3:12, 22; 1 Corinthians 6:2-3.

After the 1000-year millennial reign, of Christ the eternal order (eternity) will begin. No sin or corruption will exist ever again. Everything passes away (Revelation 21:1), and the entire universe is recreated:

Revelation 21:4-6

"And I saw a new heaven and a new earth: for the first heaven and the first earth are passed away; and the sea is no more. And I saw the holy city, New Jerusalem, coming down out of heaven from God, made ready as a bride adorned for her husband. And I heard a great voice out of the throne saying, Behold, the tabernacle of God is with men, and he shall dwell with them, and they shall be his peoples, and God himself shall be with them, and be their God."

And He shall wipe away every tear from their eyes; and death shall be no more; neither shall there be mourning, nor crying, nor pain, any more: the first things are passed away. And He that sitteth on the throne said, Behold, I make all things new. And He saith, write: for these words are faithful and true. And He said to me, they are come to pass. I am the Alpha and the Omega, the beginning and the end."

You Are Very Important to Jesus

Jeremiah 29:11-13

"For I know the thoughts I think toward you, says the LORD, thoughts of peace and not of evil, to give you a future and a hope. Then you will call upon Me and go and pray to Me, and I will listen to you. And you will seek Me and find Me, when you search for Me with all your heart."

Chapter Fourteen

Salvation Begins with Being Born-Again

Salvation through Christ Alone

"The Lord is not slack concerning His promise as some count slackness, but is longsuffering toward us, not willing that any should perish but that all should come to repentance. Nor is there salvation in any other, for there is no other name under heaven given among men by which we must be saved" (2 Peter 3:9; Acts 4:12).

Are You a Christian?

"For there is one God and one Mediator between God and men, the Man Christ Jesus, who gave Himself a ransom for all, to be testified in due time" (1 Timothy 2:5-6).

No one is born a Christian. Each person must make a conscious decision to receive Christ as Lord and Savior or reject Him. It is a choice each person on this earth must make. Vast numbers of people do not understand that the entire Bible is a Jewish book and that Christianity has Jewish roots. God used all Jewish men to pen the Bible from beginning to end, both Old and New Testaments.

The first Christians were all Jews. Jews brought the gospel to the Gentiles. And contrary to popular thinking, no one is *born* a Christian. The true meaning of what or who a Christian is has been often sorely distorted and misrepresented. Scripture teaches that each person must decide to accept or reject the truths of Christ.

God has given us free will to choose and He holds each one of us personally accountable for our acceptance or rejection of Him. Many historical and current portrayals of Christianity have nothing to do with an authentic born-again personal relationship with Jesus the Christ—which constitutes genuine Christianity as intended in the true biblical sense. For example, historically, the crusades have most often been called the "Christian Crusades." Overall, the men involved in the crusades had little or nothing to do with Christ—the Spirit of the indwelt Savior or His teachings.

The name of Jesus Christ, and the common titles: "Christian," "Christianity," and "the "Cross" are commonly assumed by those who are not at all representative of genuine Christianity, in the true biblical sense. Because of this it is easy to misidentify Jesus Christ and the true meaning of Christianity with those in our culture who carry Christ's name selfishly, inappropriately, and even diabolically to advance their own agendas.

Tremendous misinterpretation and misunderstanding exists as to just what authentic Christianity is all about and *who* Jesus Christ really is. An extreme and devastating example of how the cross has been totally twisted is by examining those who have encouraged and supported anti-Semitism. After all, Hitler was born a Roman Catholic and was never excommunicated from that church despite his horrific crimes against the Jews and humanity. By the world's standards, the Roman Catholic

Church most definitely falls directly under the umbrella of "Christianity."

A lack of awareness causes most Jews, as well as the mainstream population to identify true biblical Christianity with the Roman Catholic Church, when in fact there are some very serious, definitive differences. Most Catholics, without realizing it have been taught false doctrines that distort the true gospel message of salvation by grace alone through faith. Instead, the sixty-six books of the Bible are replaced with teachings that are steeped in mysticism, idol worship, rituals, and superstition. God's Word says that we are saved by **grace through faith** in Christ Jesus and not by our own efforts or works (Ephesians 2:8-9).

Essentially Catholic doctrine says Christ's death sacrifice is not enough, that He needs our help; when in fact it is by Christ's sacrifice on the cross, alone, and our willingness to fully accept Him by grace through faith that we are made righteous. Unfortunately, so many trusting people who are locked into the Catholic religious system are deceived and do not understand that they are participating in an apostate church that is based on unscriptural rituals and beliefs. It is a works-based religion. These same dynamics are also true for any number of religions and "Christian" denominations.

No amount of good works will ever save us. It is Christ and Christ alone who can save us. The Bible also states very clearly and unequivocally that *only* Jesus Christ can be the intercessor for the forgiveness of sins. No human, not even one wearing a shirt with a fancy collar can do the job. And no other "spirit" can save us.

How Can I Go to Heaven - What Does It Mean to Be Born-Again and Saved?

If you would like to become a true Christian by making a commitment to Jesus Christ and be born-again, the same way Yossi and his friends did at some point in their young lives, you can say the salvation prayer at the end of this chapter. Please read it before you make a commitment and also read the following Scriptures and explanations first.

Jesus Christ is the fulfillment of the prophecies of the Old Testament. He is the Messiah of the world. Jesus Christ lived a perfect sinless life on earth for us. He overcame sin for us. He died for my sins, and yours, once and for all. Jesus Christ rose from the dead. He is alive right now in heaven.

He conquered death so that you and I may have eternal life – for all those who believe in Him and are born-again. Jesus ascended into heaven where He is interceding for all born-again believers. Jesus taught that we should stop sinning and repent (turn away from). But if we do fall occasionally and sin, if we ask for forgiveness He will forgive us. But out of our love for Him we should try our best to obey His commandments.

We can do nothing to earn salvation. It is a free gift from God. Church or synagogue attendance, religious rituals and traditions – nothing else can save us except the blood of Jesus Christ — His sacrifice on the cross. Salvation is about accepting God's righteousness.

In the book of Genesis, the first book of the Bible, we learn that God created Adam and Eve in a perfect, innocent state free of sin. They both had the power to choose to obey or disobey God. When they chose to disobey God, they brought sin into God's perfect creation. It led to an overwhelming, chaotic, and devastating change in the entire scheme of creation, including the nature of Man. This is called the, "Fall of Man." Because of this, Christ came as the sacrificial Lamb to die for our sins and to reconcile us unto Himself.

Make Christ the Foundation of Your Life
Avoid Worldly Wisdom

"Let no man deceive himself. If any man among you thinks that he is wise in this age, he must become foolish, so that he may become wise. For the wisdom of this world is foolishness before God.

For it is written, "*He is* THE ONE WHO CATCHES THE WISE IN THEIR CRAFTINESS"; and again, "THE LORD KNOWS THE REASONINGS of the wise, THAT THEY ARE USELESS" (1 Corinthians 3:18-20).

We Are Reconciled to God through Salvation in Christ

"For God so loved the world that He gave His only begotten Son, that whoever believes in Him should not perish, but have everlasting life. For God did not send His Son to condemn the world, but that the world through Him might be saved" (John 3:16-17).

"Therefore, if anyone is in Christ, he is a new creation; old things have passed away; behold, all things have become new.

Now all things are of God, who has reconciled us to Himself through Jesus Christ, and has given us the ministry of reconciliation, that is, that God was in Christ reconciling the world to Himself, not imputing their trespasses to them, and has committed to us the word of reconciliation.

Now then, we are ambassadors for Christ, as though God were pleading through us: we implore you on Christ's behalf, be reconciled to God" (2 Corinthians 5:17).

We can have a personal relationship with the Lord when we come to sincere repentance and are born-again by the Holy Spirit. The spiritual rebirth Jesus spoke of is necessary in order to be saved, in order to have a personal relationship with Him and to be able to understand the Word of God through the guidance of the Holy Spirit.

Before we are saved and do not have the Holy Spirit dwelling within us, we cannot always understand the Scriptures. Those who read the Bible sporadically and never take the time to truly study it in its proper context make fun of God's holy Word and act as if those who stand in strong defense of the Bible are naïve and narrow-minded. But they are very wrong. One day every person on this earth will know that. Each person will have to stand before God one day to give an account of his or her life.

"But the natural man [unsaved person] does not receive the things of the Spirit of God, for they are foolishness to him; nor can he know them because they are spiritually discerned" (1 Corinthians 2:14).

"Jesus answered and said to him, "Truly, truly, I say to you, unless one is born-again he cannot see the kingdom of God." Nicodemus said to Him, "How can a man be born when he is old?

He cannot enter a second time into his mother's womb and be born, can he?" Jesus answered, "Truly, truly, I say to you, unless one is born of water and the Spirit, he cannot enter into the kingdom of God.

That which is born of the flesh is flesh, and that which is born of the Spirit is spirit. Do not marvel that I said to you, 'You must be born-again'" (John 3:3-7).

When we sincerely accept Christ, and receive Him as our Lord Savior, we are then immediately filled with God's Holy Spirit and are spiritually born-again. Water baptism is a public testimony showing we have placed our faith in Jesus. Being baptized as a child, a ritual performed by some religious groups will not get us into heaven.

Each person is personally accountable to God and must make his or her own decision when old enough to really understand the seriousness of the commitment – to either accept or reject God's saving grace. God gave us free will. It is up to each of us to choose eternal life with God or eternal torment and separation from God. Choose Jesus Christ and you will be saved forever. John 5:24 states:

> [Jesus said,] "Truly, truly, I say to you, he who hears My word, and believes Him who sent Me, has eternal life, and does not come into judgment, but has passed out of death into life."

Christ took on the sins of the entire world through his death on the cross to give us *all* the opportunity to be with Him for eternity and keep us from hell and the lake of fire (1 Timothy 4:10). He suffered for us, so *we* won't have to suffer an eternity of inconceivable torment.

But each individual must choose either to accept Christ by following His commandment to be "born-again," genuinely repenting and placing Him first. Or face an eternity of horror. Jesus makes references to a real hell dozens of times in the Bible.

If you are uncertain about where you will spend eternity, you can choose to place your trust in Messiah Jesus right now. Tomorrow is not promised to any one of us. Death can be a very imminent event completely out of our control. Please don't put off the most important decision of your life.

"For He made Him [Jesus] who knew no sin *to be* sin for us, that we may become the righteousness O God in Him. Behold now *is* the accepted time; behold now *is* the day of salvation" (2 Corinthians 5:21; 6b).

You can come to faith in Christ, and become born-again by praying a personal prayer of repentance and faith. The words you use are not important. Your sincerity and genuine commitment to the Lord is what counts. Saying a prayer, then walking away and forgetting about the Lord does not count for salvation.

The sincere intent of your heart is what matters to God. There has to be true *repentance*, a true change of heart so we seek Him first, and leave behind habits and lifestyles that are contrary to His will, His teachings. When we repent we turn away from the things that cause us to stumble and keep us from God's best for our lives. The Scriptures teach that true repentance will result in a change of actions (a change of mind that results in a change of actions). By our confession of faith and wholehearted belief in Jesus as Lord we are saved:

> "That if you confess, with your mouth Jesus as Lord and believe in your heart that God has raised Him from the dead, you will be saved; for with the heart man believes, resulting in righteousness, and with the mouth he confesses, resulting in salvation" (Romans 10:9-10).

If you are not sure what to say, follow this simple heartfelt prayer, but you must mean it with all your heart:

Holy Heavenly Father,

I accept Your Son, Jesus Christ, as my Lord and Savior. I believe in His death, burial and resurrection and that He lives. Forgive me for all the things I have done that are not pleasing to you. I ask you to come into my life, transform me and fill me with your Holy Spirit so I can be born-again and saved by your grace. I want this to be a new beginning and to have a close, personal relationship with you.

I want to learn more about you through prayer and careful Bible study. Help me to *truly repent* and live my life in a way that glorifies you. Please write my name into the Book of Life and count me among your righteous because of your Son's blood sacrifice and atonement on the cross. I ask this in Jesus' name. Amen.

If you have made genuine commitment to Messiah Jesus by receiving Him as your Lord and Savior, this is the most important day of your life! It is also the most significant event of your life. After all, He is now your heavenly Father (*Abba* in Hebrew), which means daddy. He wants what is best for you. Go to Him with all your concerns and pour your heart out to Him. Everything that is important to you matters to God. Nothing is too small or insignificant.

"For as many who are led by the Spirit of God, these are sons of God. For you did not receive the spirit of bondage again to fear, but you received the Spirit of adoption by whom we cry out, Abba, Father. The Spirit Himself bears witness with our spirit that we are children of God, and if children, then heirs – heirs of God and joint heirs with Christ, if indeed we suffer with Him that we may also be glorified together. For I consider that the sufferings of this present time are not worthy to be compared with the glory which shall be revealed in us" (Romans 8:14-18).

The indwelling of the Holy Spirit occurs the very moment we turn to Christ by faith (1 Corinthians 12:13). At the moment of our spiritual birth, the Spirit of God comes to live within us bringing Christ to our hearts. He then places us (spiritually baptizes us) into what is termed the body of Christ or body of Messiah (His church). He will help you understand the Scriptures

It is very important to start reading the Bible. Always pray for wisdom and understanding before beginning your Bible study. Find a quiet place away from any distractions. Many audio versions of the Bible are available to assist with the learning process. Add them to your personal library and listen to them often.

Various DVDs of movies relating to the Bible are easy to find. *Charlton Heston Presents the Bible* is a good example. Other similar DVDs can be found on the Internet or at your local Christian bookstore. Also, try to get into the practice of memorizing Scripture. Memorizing one Scripture a week is a good goal to set, say them out loud. There is power in the spoken Word of God. Let the Holy Spirit lead and teach you as you explore your Bible.

"And I will ask the Father, and He will give you another Helper, that He may be with you forever; that is the Spirit of truth, whom the world cannot receive, because it does not behold Him or know Him, but you know Him because He abides with you, and will be in you.

These things I have spoken to you, while abiding with you. But the Helper, the Holy Spirit, whom the Father will send in My name, He will teach you all things, and bring to your remembrance all that I said to you" (John 14:16, 25).

As you spend time learning more about God's Word, you will grow closer to the Lord. Prayer time and Bible study will become very important to you. Getting involved in a good Bible teaching church, a home Bible study group or a Bible based church youth group where you can have fellowship with others, can be very helpful. If you are uncertain what to do, please contact: yeshuasfriends@yahoo.com.

You Are Wonderfully Made by God

You Are Precious in the Lord's Eyes

"O LORD, You have searched me and known me. You know my sitting down and rising up; You understand my thought afar off. You comprehend my path and my lying down, and are acquainted with all my ways. For you formed my inward parts; You covered me in my mother's womb.

I will praise You, for I am fearfully and wonderfully made; marvelous are Your works, and that my soul knows very well. My frame was not hidden from You when I was made in secret, and skillfully wrought in the lowest parts of the earth.

Your eyes saw my substance being yet unformed. And in Your book they all were written, the days fashioned for me, when as yet there were none of them" (Psalm 139:1-3, 13-16).

Lay Up Treasures in Heaven

Matthew 6:19-21

"Do not lay up for yourselves treasures on earth, where moth and rust destroy and where thieves break in and steal; but lay up for yourselves treasures in heaven, where neither moth nor dust destroys and where thieves do not break in and steal. For where your treasure is, there your heart will be also."

Chapter Fifteen

What about My Life, Now That I Am Saved?

We Are Victorious in Christ

"For whatever is born of God overcomes the world. And this is the victory that has overcome the world—our faith. Who is he who overcomes the world, but he who believes that Jesus is the Son of God? But thanks be to God, who gives us the victory through our Lord Jesus Christ" (1 John 5:4-5; 1 Corinthians 15:57).

We have the promise of righteousness by grace through faith in Messiah Jesus. Salvation is through faith in Christ alone, not by any added works. Salvation is not Christ plus anything else. Whenever Man adds his own rituals and efforts to Christ's finished work on the cross, he is essentially saying what Christ did for us on the cross is not enough – that He needs our help! They are rejecting Christ's finished work on the cross.

Doing good deeds to please God is not the same as falling into a trap of performing rituals and works, implying that Christ's gift of salvation needs additional assistance in order for us to be saved and accepted into His Kingdom. This type of behavior goes directly against the Lord's teachings

Those who insist on adding their own good deeds to Christ's finished work are saying that they don't accept what Christ said when He declared: "It is finished" just before He bowed His head on the cross and gave up His Spirit (John 19:30).

We cannot improve upon what Jesus did for us when He nailed the curse of the law to the cross. He came to fulfill the law, to free us from the demands of the law found in the Old Testament of the Bible. He took all our condemnation – the curse of the law upon Himself on the cross. The entire curse of the Law of Moses was done away with when "all was fulfilled" by Christ (Luke 24:44; 2 Corinthians 3:1-18).

"For He made Him [Jesus] who knew no sin to be sin for us that we might become the righteousness of God in Him" (2 Corinthians 4:21).

We are saved by grace. Grace is God's unmerited favor. It is a gift received at Christ's expense, by blood His sacrifice on the cross. We are not justified or made holy by clinging to the law and being performance centered. We must be Christ centered. He redeemed us from the penalty of the law. We are made holy by His righteousness.

Romans 8:1-5

"There is therefore now no condemnation in Christ to those who are in Christ Jesus, who do not walk according to the flesh, but according to the Spirit. For the law of the Spirit of life in Christ Jesus has made me free from the law of sin and death.

For what the law could not do in that it was weak through the flesh, God *did* by sending His own Son in the likeness of sinful flesh, on account of sin: He condemned sin in the flesh that the righteous requirement of the law might be fulfilled in us who do not walk according to the flesh, but according to the Spirit."

When we hear the term, "falling from grace" it does not mean we fall because we are not keeping the law. Falling from grace means we are trying to *keep* the law by initiating our own rightful actions, thinking by doing so we will find favor with God to earn our way into heaven. It is especially when we fall (into sin), that the grace of God comes to our rescue! We fall from grace when we try to fulfill the law on our own merits, rejecting the grace Christ has bestowed upon all born-again believers.

"You have become estranged from Christ, you who attempt to be justified by law; you have fallen from grace. But if it is by grace, it is **no longer on the basis of works**; otherwise grace is no longer grace" (Galatians 5:4; Romans 11:6a).

We cannot earn favor with God based on *our* ability to keep the law. But the blessings of grace empower us to want to please the Lord and live to glorify Him and avoid sin. We are not justified by keeping the law. No one can keep the law perfectly. We are made righteous only by grace through faith. All the law does is show, us how badly we need our Savior, Jesus Christ – for the forgiveness of our sins.

We are made righteous by forgiveness in the blood of the sinless Son of God, not by perfect law keeping as Scripture further teaches in Romans 1:16-17; 1 Corinthians 15:1-4; 2 Corinthians 5:17; Romans 16:15-16. Christ has freed and redeemed us from the curse of law and our old flesh nature is replaced by His righteousness.

"But that no one is justified by the law in the sight of God is evident, for "the just shall live by faith." Christ has redeemed the curse of the law, having become the law, having become the curse for us.

I have been crucified with Christ; it is no longer I who live, but Christ lives in me; and the life which I now live in the flesh I live by faith in the Son of God, who loved me and gave himself for me I do not set aside the grace of God; for if righteousness comes through the law, then Christ died in vain" (Galatians 2:20-21).

"For Christ *is* the end of the law for righteousness to everyone who believes" (Romans 10:4).

Faith without Works Is Dead

Once we are saved and declared righteous in Christ by grace through faith, we show our faith and our love for Him outwardly by our actions and deeds. We are changed through salvation, by being born-again in Christ, then by walking in the Spirit of Christ dwelling within us:

> "But I say, walk in the Spirit and you shall not carry out the desire of the flesh.
>
> For the flesh sets its desire against the Spirit, and the Spirit against the flesh: for these are in opposition to one another, so that you may not do the things that you please.
>
> But if you are led by the Spirit, you are not under the Law. But the fruit of the Spirit is love, joy peace, patience, kindness, goodness, faithfulness, gentleness, self-control; against such there is no law.
>
> Now those who belong to Christ have crucified the flesh with its passions and desires. If we live by the Spirit, let us also walk in the Spirit.
>
> Let us not become boastful, challenging one another, envying one another" (Galatians 5:16, 22-26).

Chapter Sixteen

Especially for Teens and Young Adults

Christ freed us from the penalty of the law, So can we do whatever we want?

No, not at all! Jesus wants us to have a lot of fun—to enjoy our lives, but not live irresponsibly by carelessly hurting others or getting into trouble. Once we are saved we must all be careful not to use God's grace as an excuse to continue living in sin.

Christ did not die so we could habitually break basic moral guidelines. Christ's sacrifice on our behalf is not a permit to party recklessly the same way much of the unsaved world does. He wants us to be set-apart and behave with thoughtfulness and kindness, and not get caught-up with the wicked things that go on in the world. We live in a world filled with deception at every turn. What is wrong is promoted as right. What is right is much too often said to be wrong.

God's adversaries have twisted the truths of the Bible and want people to believe life is about self-gratification and self-importance. Our world is filled with the "Me" syndrome. One of the most popular songs of all-time titled, "My Way" certainly helped perpetuate the selfish sentiment. It is the same lie that caused the devil (Lucifer), once an angel of perfect beauty and wisdom to rebel against his Creator thinking he could become God. His pride caused him to fall and compete with the God of the universe. The devil has been fighting for supremacy and control ever since his he made that mistake.

God loves us and He knows what is best for us. He does not want us to get hurt. Pre-marital sex, pornography, taking drugs, drinking, smoking, swearing, wearing clothes that are too revealing and tight or sloppy, watching the perverse mind-numbing junk on TV and at the movies; all these things ultimately hurt those who are living carelessly without thinking about the end-result of their self-destructive lifestyles. Keep yourself as pure as possible in what you allow yourself to do, what you look at and what you allow yourself to hear.

Peer pressure to become popular and be part of the crowd can be overwhelming, but when you get hurt or get into trouble, you will be on your own and those "friends" who are pushing you to do questionable things will not be the ones reaping the consequences of risky behavior, it will be you. And if you are very young and still going through high school or middle school understand that most of your classmates now will not even be part of your future because as you get older you will make new friends—another good reason not to let those around you right sway you into doing things that you will regret. Most of the people you know now in school will become a distant memory, so never mind if they treat you like an outcast if you refuse to go along with their bad behavior and wicked schemes.

Learn the following Scripture found in the letter (epistle) that the apostle Paul wrote to the Galatians. Use it as a guide to help you stay true to God's desire for you to have His very best for your life:

"Now the deeds of the flesh are evident, which are: immorality, impurity, sensuality, idolatry, sorcery, enmities, strife, jealousy, outbursts of anger, disputes, dissensions, factions, envying, drunkenness, carousing, and things like these, of which I forewarn you, just as I have forewarned you, that those who practice such things will not inherit the kingdom of God" (Galatians 5:19-21).

Yossi and his friends had to battle the forces of darkness. It is the same for us. This world is filled with agents of the devil trying to cause us to fall away from the truths of God. We are living in a spiritual war zone each and every day. Deception is the devil's primary weapon. Choose to be on God's side, not the losing side. Just because something looks good on the surface does not mean it is really good.

Satan appeared in various forms to Michael and Gabriel when they were trying to fix the problems with demonic strongholds in the story you just read. It was noted that the Bible teaches how the devil can appear as an angel of light (2 Corinthians 11:14) and fool us into thinking what he is offering is good.

As long as we are alive and live in this fleshly body, even after we are saved we will be tempted to sin against God – due to the sinful human nature we inherited when Adam and Eve yielded to temptation. But we can avoid obvious circumstances that will hurt us and cause us to sin. When we are truly saved we are born of the Spirit of God, filled with the Holy Spirit, and we can walk in the Spirit of God's strength in a heart of obedience wanting to please Him.

Satan uses all kinds of people and situations to help him with his dirty work. Don't let yourself become one of his casualties. He is very active in this world and his agenda is to ruin as many lives as possible. Be like Yossi and his friends, be a Defender of the Faith! Don't let yourself be hoodwinked by the devil when he uses the glitz and glitter of this world to tempt you. Choose your role models very carefully.

"And do not be conformed to this world, but be transformed by the renewing of your mind, that you may prove what is that good and acceptable and perfect will of God" (Romans 12:2).

"No temptation has overtaken you but such as is common to man; and God is faithful, who will not allow you to be tempted beyond what you are able, but with the temptation will provide the way of escape also, so that you will be able to endure it" (1 Corinthians 10:13).

What Will My Friends Think?

"Let no one despise your youth, but be an example to the believers in word, in conduct, in love, in spirit, in faith, in purity" (1 Timothy 4:12).

Set yourself apart from the "popular" crowd and be popular with Jesus instead. Live to please Christ, not so-called friends who want to take you down destructive roads and away from the truths of the Bible. God has a plan for your life. He has the right friends, the right girl or right guy out there for you. Spend your time learning and studying the Scriptures. Grow close to Jesus and He will guide you every day.

Instead of watching mind-numbing television shows and playing video games that are packed with damaging, violent anti-biblical themes or reading popular magazines that promote vulgarity, loose morals and racy trendy fashion trends, fill your mind with the Holy Spirit empowered God-given Scriptures and biblically related entertainment. Find others who love the Lord. Make new friends you can respect and spend time with them. Doing these things will enable you to grow spiritually and emotionally and you will be ready to face life's challenges.

One day when you look back at your life you will be glad you did not waste your time wandering aimlessly with those who are not serving God. Some people you might think have a lot going for them—those who are considered popular and successful by the world's standards could very well be the last people you will want to be around as you continue to spiritually grow; as you walk closer with the Lord.

Jesus promises a glorious future for all those who belong to Him. Isn't it better to know you will spend eternity with the King of the universe who favors you and loves you beyond comprehension than to try to please people who have no long-term interest in your happiness and well-being?

Choosing true born-again friends is especially important in dating and marriage relationships. Dating is something that should be done very cautiously and not often. It is much better to cultivate true Christian friendships and by doing so you will meet the right companion that God has in mind for you. Once you become a born-again believer being romantically involved with a non-Christian is a sure recipe for pain and heartache. A divided house cannot stand. It will be very wobbly at best. God tells us not to make this painful mistake. Trust that this is very important advice from your heavenly Father.

"Do not be unequally yoked together with unbelievers. For what fellowship has righteousness with lawlessness? And what communion has light with darkness? And what accord has Christ with Belial? Or what part has a believer with an unbeliever? And what agreement has the temple of God with idols?" (2 Corinthians 6:14-16).

The following Scripture is important to focus on, to hold close to your heart as you begin your new life in Christ.

"Not that I have already attained, or am already perfected; but I press on, that I may lay hold of that for which Christ Jesus has also laid hold of me. Brethren, I do not count myself to have apprehended; but one thing *I do,* **forgetting those things which** are **behind** and **reaching forward** to those things which are ahead, I press toward the goal for the prize of the upward call of God in Christ Jesus" (Philippians 3:12-14).

Earlier I mentioned we must be careful not to use the grace of God as an open door to recklessly fall into a sinful lifestyle. Through God's grace, the Holy Spirit comes to live in us when we make a true commitment to Christ, when we are born-again.

He works in us giving us the ability to pull back from sin. God is against sin because it hurts us, and sometimes totally destroys the lives of more people than we can count. Humanity has been on a downward spiral for thousands of years because of sin. We do not have the ability in our own strength to never sin, and then reverse its effects. It is God's grace that covers and erases sin in our lives. It is when we are covered by His grace and we yield to the power of the Holy Spirit, that sin loses its power of control over us.

The apostle Paul wrote about how sin will no longer dominate us once we are saved by God's grace. "What shall we say then? Shall we continue in sin that grace may abound? Certainly not! For if we have been united together in the likeness of His death, certainly we also shall be *in the likeness* of His resurrection, knowing this, that our old man was crucified with Him, that the body of sin might be done away with, that we should no longer be slaves to sin. Therefore do not let sin reign in your mortal body, that you should obey its lusts. For sin shall have no dominion over you, for you are not under law but under grace" (Romans 6:1-2, 5-7, 12, 14).

"But now we have been released from the Law, having died to that by which we were bound, **so that we serve in newness of the Spirit** and not in oldness of the letter" (Romans 7:6).

If we are to be genuinely "not of this world" as Scripture teaches, then we should do our best to take on the values that Jesus had. It means that we must truly care about others, appreciate all our blessings, live a balanced life, place God first in our lives and die to the old nature that wants to control everything. Let Jesus take the driver's seat and you will find you will have a much better, more abundant life. No one in this life can be free of trials and tribulations, but when we belong to Christ He will strengthen us and carry our burdens. Be encouraged, and know that all things are possible in Christ Jesus. He is the great I Am, Who Was, Is and ever shall be.

"For with God nothing will be impossible. I can do all things through Christ who strengthens me" (Luke 1:37; Philippians 4:13).

Jesus is the best friend we could ever hope for. He loves us enough to have suffered a brutal death for us so we can have eternal life and be saved from the horrors of hell; so we can live with Him forever and ever—in the most awesome place of indescribable beauty and joy. Don't let the short-term worldly temptations—the lies of this world—keep you from an eternity with God. Eternity is a very, very long time.

[Jesus said,] "These things I have I have spoken to you, that in Me you may have peace. In this world you will have tribulation; but be of good cheer, for I have overcome the world. "Come to Me, all you who labor and are heavy laden, and I will give you rest. For my yoke is easy and my burden is light" (John 16:33).

Think on Virtuous Things

"Finally, brethren, whatever things are true, whatever things *are* noble, whatever things *are* just, whatever things *are* pure, whatever things *are* lovely, whatever things *are* of good report, if *there is* any virtue and if *there is* anything praiseworthy—meditate on these things. The things which you learned and received and heard and saw in me, these do, and the God of peace will be with you" (Philippians 4:8-9).

Holiness and Purity Are a Blessing

Holiness and purity should be something everyone strives for on a daily basis, especially professing Christians. We should do this for many reasons. Here are some reasons why all believers in Jesus, Yeshua the Messiah, should strive to live a holy life:

Gratitude for the love of our Father: He gave His only begotten Son for us.

"But God demonstrates His own love toward us, in that while we were yet sinners, Christ died for us" (Romans 5:8).

Gratitude for the love of Jesus (Yeshua): He voluntarily died for us.

"I am the good shepherd; the good shepherd lays down His life for the sheep" (John 10:11).

Gratitude for the cleansing of our sins and for eternal life: Jesus died for us. He suffered the most excruciating death imaginable to pay the price for our sins, and He took the punishment for our sins in His body while He hung on the cross. He then rose from the tomb to give us eternal life.

"And from Jesus Christ, the faithful witness, the firstborn of the dead, and the ruler over the kings of the earth. To Him who loves us and washed us from our sins by His blood" (Revelation 1:5).

Rewards: When we live a holy life for the Lord obeying His commands and doing His will we will receive eternal rewards for our service.

"Now if anyone builds on this foundation with gold, silver, precious stones, wood, hay, straw, each one's work will become clear; for the Day will declare it, because it will be revealed by fire; and the fire will test each one's work, of what sort it is. If anyone's work which he has built on it endures, he will receive a reward" (1 Corinthians 3:12-14).

Obedience: We are commanded to be holy.

"But as He who called you *is* holy, you also be holy in all *your* conduct, because it is written, "Be holy, for I am holy" (1 Peter 1:15-16).

Choose to live a holy life that brings glory and honor to God, which will result in hearing that coveted praise from Him when we go home to live with Him forever and are face to face with Him:

"His lord said to him, 'Well *done,* good and faithful servant; you have been faithful over a few things, I will make you ruler over many things. Enter into the joy of your lord'" (Matthew 25:23).

Holiness comes at a cost. Instead of fulfilling our desires of the flesh, eyes and the boastful pride of life we will use our time to get to know our Lord and Savior through daily prayer and daily Bible reading, study, memorization and meditating on the teachings of Holy Bible. As we immerse ourselves in continual prayer and reading of the Word we will be transformed from the inside out:

"I beseech you therefore, brethren, by the mercies of God, that you present your bodies a living sacrifice, holy, acceptable to God, *which is* your reasonable service. And do not be conformed to this world, but be transformed by the renewing of your mind, that you may prove what *is* that good and acceptable and perfect will of God" (Romans 12:1-2).

It is the Word of God that helps cleanse us of our sinful desires and gives us the strength to live holy lives:

"That he might sanctify and cleanse her [the church] with the washing of water by the word" (Ephesians 5:26).

A good relationship with God depends on right relationships with others. If we do not have a right relationship with others, then our relationship with God is affected. When we pray and bathe ourselves in His Word God gives us the strength to live a holy life for Him, which also benefits our relationships with others.

Begin with the basics: Pray throughout each day, read a few chapters each day. If you read four chapters a day you will read through the entire Bible once each year. Choose a book of the Bible to study and then work through it a little each day. If you need workbooks to help you study, use them. Also set up a memorization program—one verse a month, a week or one a day, whichever you can handle and hide God's Word in your heart. This is a vital part of living a holy and pure life:

"How can a young man keep his way pure? By keeping it according to Your word. With all my heart I have sought You; do not let me wander from Your commandments. Your word I have treasured in my heart, that I may not sin against You" (Psalm 119:9-11).

The choice is yours. Choose to serve God—Jesus Christ the Savior, or yourself. Chose Christ and in Him you will be victorious no matter what happens in this world (1 Corinthians 15:57). When you chose Christ you will spend eternity with Him and will not be left on earth to experience the Tribulation years.

"If it is disagreeable in your sight to serve the LORD, choose for yourselves today whom you will serve: whether the gods which your fathers served which were beyond the River, or the gods of the Amorites in whose land you are living; but as for me and my house, we will serve the LORD" (Joshua 24:15).

Purity

Two sins, which cause a great many believers to stumble, are riches and sex. Please give these exhortations from God's Word careful consideration:

> "But those who want to get rich fall into temptation and a snare and many foolish and harmful desires which plunge men into ruin and destruction. For the love of money is a root of all sorts of evil, and some by longing for it have wandered away from the faith and pierced themselves with many griefs" (1 Timothy 6:9-11).

Instead of seeking after riches, which can vanish in an instant through a bad investment, theft or an economic or natural catastrophe, we should pursue righteousness, godliness, faith, love, perseverance and gentleness. Sex outside of marriage is a sin, which few believers seem to escape. But in Christ, in His strength we can escape all temptations. Study these passages and meditate on them night and day. Sex outside of marriage is a very serious offense to God and to one self:

> "Do you not know that your bodies are members of Christ? Shall I then take away the members of Christ and make them members of a prostitute? May it never be! Or do you not know that the one who joins himself to a prostitute is one body with her?

For He says, "THE TWO SHALL BECOME ONE FLESH." But the one who joins himself to the Lord is one spirit with Him. Flee immorality. Every other sin that a man commits is outside the body, but the immoral man sins against his own body" (1 Corinthians 6:15-18).

Sexual relations outside of marriage, always leads to shame and humiliation as Solomon explained:

"The one who commits adultery with a woman is lacking sense; he who would destroy himself does it. Wounds and disgrace he will find, and his reproach will not be blotted out. For jealousy enrages a man, and he will not spare in the day of vengeance. He will not accept any ransom, nor will he be satisfied though you give many gifts" (Proverbs 6:32-35).

Many well-known pastors have humiliated themselves, their families and God Almighty by committing adultery. The long-term ramifications of the shame and humiliation far out-weigh the brief satisfaction derived from those affairs. There can never be any justification for it. Instead of seeking to satisfy our petty desires of the flesh—no matter what they may be, let us seek to do all we can to bring glory to God, because He lives inside of us:

"Or do you not know that your body is a temple of the Holy Spirit who is in you, whom you have from God, and that you are not your own? For you have been

bought with a price: therefore glorify God in your body"
(1 Corinthians 6:19-20).

Another problem prevalent today is seeing celebrities setting ungodly examples having babies outside of marriage. These women parade around as if true commitment is irrelevant when bringing children into the world. It is as if having a baby outside the marriage covenant is a badge of honor proving some sort of self-indulgent point. And then the shocked masses wonder why these celebrities breakdown emotionally or overdose on drugs. Of course this way of life trickles down to the rest of society. Instead of having strong bonded-families we find broken-lives and the children suffer the most. (Just what the devil ordered and loves.)

The morality in the culture has broken down to a point where living together without marriage is considered the "norm." Even some older folks—grandparents who are divorced or have been widowed, no longer abide by God's marriage covenant, but instead, move in together (shack up). This type of behavior sets a very poor example for their children, grandchildren and the rest of society. But few people seem to care. But God cares and He is righteous God.

"The thief does not come except to steal, and to kill, and to destroy" (John 10:10a).

The entire moral climate of this world is falling lower day by day. These lost souls are playing right into the devil's plans to destroy families, ruin the lives of as many people as possible and keep individuals from coming to salvation in Christ. "If it feels good do it" was a slogan in the 1960s era. Today, it is a "given" regardless of the damaging consequences of this type of selfish reckless, "It feels good so do it," behavior.

Something that is quite astounding is when mothers of teenagers try to dress like they are going out on the town to hit the dance clubs and bars, wearing tight short-shorts, and short skimpy tops revealing their stomach flab, their faces plastered with garish make-up strutting around as if they are onto something very "cool."

I have seen this pathetic display of middle-aged vulgarity even at the local supermarkets. I feel sorry for the children of these mothers. If the mother, as a role model looks this disgraceful what chance does the daughter or son have to look, and behave in a godly manner?

Abstinence Is Powerful

Remember, as a born-again believer the Holy Spirit lives inside you and you are hurting Him as well as yourself if you get involved in a sexual relationship outside the marriage covenant. Abstinence may not be popular by the world's standards but you are worth far more than the "here today, gone tomorrow" attitudes of those who are blindly stumbling through life. Chastity is a wonderful quality.

Stay away from those who want to cause you to compromise godly values. Sexual promiscuity destroys the moral fiber of a person and leaves many scars. Stay close to Jesus, always pray for protection from evil (often disguised as "fun") and you will be greatly blessed.

Value God's Special Blessings

What a treasure it is to save your most intimate-self for the special one that God has in mind for you. Promiscuity, in this morally depraved culture has become the norm but carries with it lifelong heartaches. Choose to rise above the crowd and walk away from any type of relationship that entices you to engage in sexual relations outside a strong marriage bond. Choose wisely who you spend time with and who you trust.

Choose your friends carefully. It is better to have one good friend you can trust instead of a room full of "party" types who do not care anything about you and have no respect for themselves, either. Find friends who love the Lord and that you can share your faith with. If you find yourself feeling lonely and like the whole world is falling apart around you because of the overwhelming negativity and wretched moral standards, realize that all true born-again believers are promised a wonderful future in a place where only the King Jesus will rule and all the disappointments you may be feeling now will be gone forever.

This is not our true home. This world is very temporary and we are getting closer each day to the Lord's soon return. Be sure you belong to Him and you are guaranteed by God Himself to have a glorious eternal future. Keep your heart and mind focused on Jesus and He will carry you through any challenge. Let Him be your best friend.

Especially for the Young Ladies

I know of a young woman, Elizabeth, raised by a godly mother. She grew-up reading the Bible and was taught how to behave in an orderly, respectful manner. When she was still a young teen, a group of girls from her school invited her to a get-together one evening. Her friends had managed to gather together some alcohol and were ready to tell some lies to their parents so they could stay up all night.

The girls planned to go out and about town to bars and night-clubs wearing very short tight skirt, high heels and flashy over-done make-up. They even had a very short skirt and a pair of high-heeled shoes set-aside for Elizabeth. These rebellious and confused teens thought the seductive ads in all the magazines were the thing to follow.

Elizabeth had no idea that her friends had planned a night of trouble. She told them she would not lie to her mother and would not participate in their devious sordid little plan to go out carousing all night long around town. She urged them not to go out and place themselves in harm's way. From that point on those "friends" treated Elizabeth very rudely and deliberately snubbed her at school and around town.

She also wisely knew that dressing seductively and cheaply would do nothing but hurt her and attract the wrong type of admirers. All the magazines that promote risqué clothing and loose living are breaking down the moral fiber of society while making lots of money for themselves and their advertisers. Since Elizabeth had a good, solid foundation in Christ she stood by her principles.

Years later the girls who thought they were so "cool" all got into some kind of trouble and regretted their wild reckless behavior. But Elizabeth went on to college and made some good Christian friends, met a very special guy who also loves the Lord and is now her best friend. She is well-grounded in the Lord and on her way to achieving a meaningful purpose in her life. She is about to get a marriage proposal. Elizabeth is the girl to emulate, not her confused and devious former girlfriends.

Today's culture does very little to show a young woman how to behave like a young lady, with the rare exception of the mentoring from a caring parent, family member, teacher or friend. Few role models exist today who act ladylike. Even some women who call themselves Bible believing Christians use crass, foul language and tell off-color "jokes."

And I have seen women who are professing Christians publicly guzzle wine, glass after glass only to order an entire bottle and continue drinking. This type of behavior cheapens women and weakens their testimony for Christ. And some wear clothes that make them look more masculine than feminine, or dress like harlots instead of ladies. I have seen immodest inappropriate clothing worn even at some popular churches.

Don't be fooled by the false glamour and sizzle woven into the culture in the form of magazines and various types of advertising, showcasing provocative distasteful clothing, and overdone make-up techniques that take away from the natural beauty of a woman. Keep your lifestyle simple, wear lovely clothing that is in good taste and reflects the beauty of God's creation—you!

Especially for the Guys

Contrary to the in-your-face worldly propaganda, women also like to have a man who is not a run-around promiscuous type. Respect goes both ways. If you want the right kind of woman to respect you, then behave responsibly with dignity and valor. Be chivalrous and kind. Save yourself for your future wife and don't get caught-up in the worldly dating and party scene. And the sloppy "look" does nothing for any man—young or old, so don't follow the trends especially wearing oversized clothes that look like they are falling off you—forcing you to walk like some sort of loser.

When the timing is right, God will send you the right woman to spend the rest of your life with. The most attractive thing to a woman of all ages is a generous man who places the needs of others before his own, not someone who complains about having to work for a living or someone who does little or nothing to improve the quality of life for his family. The well-being and welfare of a man's wife and children should come before his own.

No one likes a self-centered bully who cares primarily about himself and overreacts to every little thing for no good reason. One of the worst things you can do is speak harshly to your wife and children. A person who overreacts by shouting and yelling, instead of speaking calmly, is a person who has no self-control and has never grown-up.

All that is accomplished and created by this type of childish behavior is a stressful atmosphere in the home where no one will dare speak a word for fear of being admonished; all because of one self-righteous bully. And trying to prove how many beers you can slug down, is hardly the sign of manhood, it is a sign of stupidity and irresponsibility. Countless families have been ruined by the abusive behavior of immature self-centered people. Instead of being the spiritual leader God calls men to be, too many act like troubled adolescents. This is also true for some women, but it seems that men are strongly leading in this area.

Women want a man that they can depend on and lean on, a trusted protector, someone who will do whatever it takes to provide the best life possible for his family. Be a gentleman, be generous, caring and thoughtful and you will be a happy man. If you make a woman feel really cared for, and do anything you can to make her life in this fallen world, better, then you will have her love and loyalty forever. Learn the following verse and when you follow this principle, your future wife will do anything she can to please you, too.

"Husbands, love your wives, just as Christ also loved the church and gave Himself for her" (Ephesians 5:23a).

The following verse teaches that if a man is not considerate and respectful of his wife, his prayers will be hindered. If a husband does not treat his wife with the love, honor, and respect that she deserves, his prayers are not very effective. It is beneficial to get into good habits and understand God's principles and expectations long before taking marriage vows.

"Husbands, in the same way be considerate as you live with your wives, and treat them with respect as the weaker partner and as heirs with you of the gracious gift of life, so that nothing will hinder your prayers" (1 Peter 3:7).

Encouragement for Everyone

If you have regrets and have made some mistakes (we all have) you can repent and God will heal your emotional wounds. We cannot undo the past but in Christ we are a new creation and all things are new. Because of Him you will become righteous and pure in His eyes. Vow to only engage in physical relations with a lifelong partner sealed *first* with God's marriage covenant. Realize once you are saved and born-again by the Spirit of God you get your identity from Christ, not from the clothes you wear or the type of car you drive or who your friends are.

Becoming born-again in Christ totally frees you from the world's entrapments. You are totally sufficient in Christ. Nothing in this world can make you whole other than the Lord Jesus. A personal relationship with Him truly is the answer to all problems, including those painful low self-worth issues that the world just loves to fill our minds with. Jesus is the Great Physician who heals us from the wounds inflicted by the world.

God has the right person in mind for you. He or she will be so glad you did not compromise yourself, and so will you. Never mind what your friends are doing. You may feel lonely sometimes, but that is when you can go to the Lord and spend time with Him. He will strengthen you to remain pure. What matters is that you do your best to follow God's principles. He has your best interests at heart. When temptation comes your way, God will always make a way out. And practice saying, "No." :)

"Be not deceived: Evil companionships corrupt good morals" (1 Corinthians 15:33).

In Christ You Are a New Creation

"But you have not so learned Christ, if indeed you have heard Him and have been taught by Him, as the truth is in Jesus: that you put off, concerning your former conduct, the old man which grows corrupt according to the deceitful lusts, and be renewed in the spirit of your mind, and that you put on the new man which was created according to God, in true righteousness and holiness" (Ephesians 4:20-24).

Let Go of the Past

"Not that I have already attained, or am already perfected; but I press on, that I may lay hold of that for which Christ Jesus has also laid hold of me. Brethren, I do not count myself to have apprehended; but one thing *I do,* forgetting those things which are behind and reaching forward to those things which are ahead, I press toward the goal for the prize of the upward call of God in Christ Jesus" (Philippians 3:12-14).

Chapter Seventeen

Prayer–Take the Humble Approach

Matthew 6:5-8

[Jesus said] "And when you pray, you shall not be like the hypocrites; for they love to pray standing in the synagogues and on the corners of the streets, that they may be seen by men.

Assuredly, I say to you, they have their reward. But when you pray, go into your room, and when you have shut your door, pray to your Father who is in the secret place; and your Father who sees in secret will reward you openly.

And when you pray, do not use vain repetitions as the heathen do, for. For they think that they will be heard for their many words. Therefore do not be like them, for your Father knows the things you have need of before you ask Him."

It is very important to pray daily and often. Prayer is our communication line to God, as are the Holy Scriptures—the Bible. Talk to Him about everything. He loves us completely – in ways we cannot begin to understand and is interested in the matters that concern us. He knows everything there is to know about us, but nevertheless wants to have an ongoing personal communication with us.

Scripture teaches that the Lord even knows how many hairs are numbered on our heads (Luke 12:7, Matthew 10:30) and that He collects our tears in a bottle and keeps a written record of them (Psalm 56:8). Reach out to Him and He will guide and comfort you. He will make a way for you when there seems no way.

"Be anxious for nothing, but in everything by prayer and supplication with thanksgiving let your requests be made known to God. And the peace of God, which surpasses all comprehension, shall guard your hearts and your minds in Christ Jesus" (Philippians 4:6-7).

The Word of God, the Bible, teaches us to pray to the Father in Jesus' name (John 14:13-14). Prayer is one of the many basic daily activities of all believers. Reading, hearing, studying and contemplating Scripture are the other basic daily activities. We should pray several times a day. We are encouraged to pray always (Ephesians 6:18; 1 Thessalonians 5:17).

We have the example of Paul (Colossians 1:3; 2 Timothy 1:3). In Scripture we have the example of Timothy (Colossians 1:3). Praying always means to be in constant communication with the Lord. We can make brief requests and express our gratitude while we are on the go and we should pray privately on our knees as the Lord and the apostles did (Mark 14:32-35; 6:12; 22:41; Ephesians 3:14; Acts 7:60; 9:40; 20:36; 21:5).

We should pray in the Holy Spirit (Ephesians 6:18; Jude 20, Romans 8:26), and pray according to the will of God (1 John 5:14-15).

If we are unsure what to pray, we can pray in the Holy Spirit as taught in Romans 8:26: "Likewise the Spirit also helps in our weaknesses. For we do not know what we should pray for as we ought, but the Spirit Himself makes intercession for us with groaning, which cannot be uttered." Believers can know God's will by studying the Scriptures. Prayer is our way of speaking to the Lord. He speaks to us through His Word. It is a blessing to hear, read, study, and memorize His Word every day, to listen to Him. When we pray and seek the Lord, the Holy Spirit will guide us in our daily lives. Listen to His "still small voice" nudging within, His gentle push to gain your attention or give a signal. This is not to be confused with what the world calls "intuition." The Holy Spirit is a real Person actively guiding the faithful believer.

Types of Prayer

The three types of prayer are praise, intercession (when we pray on the behalf of others) and personal requests. These three types of prayer can be short prayers or lengthy ones. It is a blessing to be devoted to prayer (Romans 12:12; Colossians 4:2; 1 Peter 4:7); meaning we should spend time in private prayer on our knees, and in prayer when on the go. We should also pray with others (Acts 1:3, 16:25).

Do Good to Please God
Not to Impress Others

When you feel compelled to give to others it is always best not to go around announcing and bragging about your good deeds. Give generously but be sure your motives are pure. If you give, give out of love not to get adulation from others.

Matthew 6:1-4

"Take heed that you do not do your charitable deeds before men, to be seen by them. Otherwise you have no reward from your Father in heaven. Therefore when you do a charitable deed, do not sound a trumpet before you as the hypocrites do in the synagogues and in the streets, that they may have glory from men.

Assuredly, I say to you, they have their reward. But when you do a charitable deed, do not let your left hand know what your right hand is doing, that your charitable deed may be in secret; and your Father who sees in secret will Himself reward you openly."

What Happens When We Pray Together?

[Jesus said,] "Assuredly, I say to you, whatever you bind on earth will be bound in heaven, and whatever you loose on earth will be loosed in heaven. Again I say to you that if two of you agree on earth concerning anything that they ask, it will be done for them by My Father in heaven. For where two or three are gathered together in My name, I am there in the midst of them" (Matthew 18:18-20).

Forgiveness Is God's Way

"Pride goes before destruction, and a haughty spirit
before a fall" (Proverbs 16:18).

The Lord forgives each one of us for all our inequities, and we
are asked to do the same. No matter how much we have been
hurt or are falsely accused and how unbearable it might feel, we
must forgive. We cannot truly grow as believers if we harbor
animosity toward others in our hearts. We should never harden
our hearts toward others. It is not always an easy thing to do, but
with God we can forgive those who have wronged us and live a
more abundant life in Christ.

If you have wronged someone and have offered an apology
but your apology or effort to mend the situation is rejected, if
you feel so inclined you can go to that person with other believers and try to resolve the problem. If they do not respond kindly,
then you have done all you can and you must let go of the situation and that person. If someone has wronged you and instead
of making amends continues to attack and slander you, then rest
assured that God Himself will deal with the situation and expose
the truth.

"Moreover if your brother sins against you, go and tell
him his fault between you and him alone. If he hears you,
you have gained your brother. But if he will not hear, take
with you one or two more, than by the mouth of two or
three witnesses every word may be established. And if

he refuses to hear them, tell it to the church. But if he refuses even to hear the church, let him be to you like a heathen and a tax collector" (Matthew 18:15-17).

[Jesus said,] "But I say to you, love your enemies, bless those who curse you, do good to those who hate you, and pray for those who spitefully use you and persecute you" (Matthew 5:44).

A benefit of forgiveness is being at peace within ourselves knowing that we have forgiven those who have harmed us and we are not carrying a grudge. That does not mean we have to let those same offenders run all over us or get deeply involved with them. Forgiveness does not equal foolishness. When the unkind motives and attitudes of a person are exposed you can fully forgive them in your heart but move on and pray for them to come to repentance. Only if the offender truly repents can an authentic relationship be resumed.

Many Christians are wonderful caring individuals but not all professing Christians are genuine. How a person acts toward others, especially in the area of forgiveness is a real test of just who, and what they really are. If we don't have a right relationship with people, we cannot have a right relationship with God. This is a serious problem with some so-called Christians who behave unkindly and self-righteously. Those who place self-centered demands on other believers do nothing good for the body of Christ. They cause division and place undue pressure on others.

It is shocking to find some disturbed individuals who call themselves Christians afflicted with the need to control, and have power over others. This is a very sad testimony to the world, and especially newcomers to the faith. No wonder some people want nothing to do with anyone called a "Christian." The best thing to do is not get involved with these types of people. Such individuals should not partake in any ministry until they wholeheartedly repent and get right with the Lord. Making excuses for those who call themselves Christians but verbally attack and work to undermine others, is not doing them a favor. It is enabling them to continue to fall from grace.

[Jesus said,] "For if your forgive men for their transgressions, your heavenly Father will also forgive you. But if you do not forgive men, then your Father will not forgive your transgressions" (Matthew 6:14-15).

Chapter Eighteen

The Judgment Seat of Christ

All believers after they are taken in the Rapture will stand before the Lord in what is often termed as the Bema Seat of Christ or the Judgment Seat of Christ:

> "For we must all appear before the Judgment Seat of Christ, that each one may be recompensed for his deeds in the body, according to what he has done, whether good or bad" (2 Corinthians 5:10).

The Scripture above is referring to believers, not the unsaved. Unbelievers who die in their sins without accepting Christ's free gift of salvation will face the Great White Throne Judgment immediately after the one-thousand-year millennial reign of Christ. The Judgment Seat of Christ takes place after the Rapture, and involves believers giving an account of their lives face to face with Messiah Jesus—all those whose names are found in the Book of Life.

The Judgment Seat of Christ does not determine our salvation. We know that was resolved forever by His sacrifice on the cross on our behalf (1 John 2:2 and John 3:16). All born-again believers' sins are forgiven, and they will never be condemned or judged for them (Romans 8:1). Also, at the Judgment Seat of Christ rewards will be given to believers based on how steadfastly and faithfully we serve Him (1 Corinthians 9:4-27) and (2 Timothy 2:5).

The motives for everything a believer does for the Lord will be judged. Some will lose their rewards because their motives for serving the Lord are insincere and self-serving (1 Corinthians 3:10-15). Or those who may think they are serving the Lord will find out that they have been stubborn and headstrong, unwilling to seriously search the Scriptures and admit errors in teaching and repent.

Accountability for our faithfulness to the Lord and His Scriptures, not the approval of our core group of friends will determine our rewards or loss of them (1 Corinthians 3:11-15).

Crowns will be given for different reasons based on how faithfully the Lord was served. The crowns are described in 2 Timothy 4:8; 2 Timothy 2:5; James 1:12; 1 Peter 5:4; Revelation 2.

The Great White Throne Judgment

"Jesus said to him, 'I am the way, the truth, and the life. No one comes to the Father, except through Me.' And there is salvation in no one else; for there is no other name under heaven that has been given among men, by which we must be saved" (John 14:6; Acts 4:12).

"For it is written, as I live, saith the Lord, to me every knee shall bow, and every tongue shall confess to God. So then each one of us shall give account of himself to God" (Romans 14:11-12).

Immediately after the one-thousand-year millennial kingdom, the Great White Throne Judgment will take place when everyone who died in their sins is judged—those who never accepted Messiah Jesus as Savior and Lord. It will be too late for salvation in Christ for those who did not want to receive the truth while they were still alive. And for those who worshiped other gods and did not fully accept Christ as the one and only way to the Father in heaven.

In the following Scripture we learn that those who die in their sins without accepting Christ's free gift of salvation will actually be judged from a written record found in books and "according to their works" (Revelation 20:12).

Revelation 20:13-15

"And the sea gave up the dead that were in it; and death and Hades gave up the dead who were in them: and they were judged every man according to their works. And death and Hades were cast into the lake of fire. This is the second death, *even* the lake of fire. And if any was not found written in the Book of Life, he was cast into the lake of fire."

The Eternal Kingdom

After the Great White Throne Judgment, the eternal kingdom will begin. No sin or corruption will exist ever again. Everything passes away (Revelation 21:1), and the entire universe is recreated:

Revelation 21:4-6

"And I saw a new heaven and a new earth: for the first heaven and the first earth are passed away; and the sea is no more. And I saw the holy city, New Jerusalem, coming down out of heaven from God, made ready as a bride adorned for her husband.

And I heard a great voice out of the throne saying, Behold, the tabernacle of God is with men, and he shall dwell with them, and they shall be his peoples, and God himself shall be with them, *and be* their God.

And He shall wipe away every tear from their eyes; and death shall be no more; neither shall there be mourning, nor crying, nor pain, any more: the first things are passed away. And He that sitteth on the throne said, Behold, I make all things new. And He saith, write: for these words are faithful and true. And He said to me, they are come to pass. I am the Alpha and the Omega, the beginning and the end."

The Lord has a special place throughout eternity for the Jewish people. Scripture teaches that upon walking into the holy

City of the New Jerusalem, individuals will have to walk under and over the name of a Jew:

> "And he carried me away in the Spirit to a mountain great and high, and showed me the holy city Jerusalem, coming down out of heaven from God, having the glory of God: her light was like unto a stone most precious, as it were jasper stone, clear as crystal; having a wall great and high; having twelve gates, and at the gates twelve angels; and names written theron, which are *the names* of the twelve tribes of the children of Israel" (Revelation 21:10-12).

The eternal city—the New Jerusalem will have streets of pure gold, clear like glass and phenomenal jewel laden gates and walls. The city will not have or need the light of the sun or the moon because the Lamb—the Lord Jesus, will be the light (Revelation 21:23). Revelation 21:24 shows that new nations will be created for the eternal kingdom that will glorify the Lord. Their inhabitants will not be sinful beings:

Revelation 21:22-27

> "And I saw no temple in it, for the Lord God, the Almighty, and the Lamb are its temple. And the city has no need of the sun or the moon to shine upon it, for the glory of God has illumed it, and its lamp *is* the Lamb. And the nations shall walk by its light, and the kings of the earth shall bring their glory into it.

And in the daytime (for there shall be no night there) its gates shall never be closed. And they shall bring the glory and the honor of the nations to it; and nothing unclean and no one who practices abomination and lying, shall ever come to it, but only those whose names are written in the Lamb's Book of Life."

Perfection and exquisite beauty will be found everywhere in the Lord's eternal kingdom. Any dream or imagined thought we might have of a perfect world will seem utterly insignificant when compared to the magnificent glory of the Lord and His eternal provisions. The apostle John describes more as we read on into Revelation 22.1-5:

"Then he showed me a river of the water of life, clear as crystal, coming from the throne of God and of the Lamb, in the middle of its street. On either side of the river was the tree of life, bearing twelve *kinds of* fruit, yielding its fruit every month; and the leaves of the tree were for the healing of the nations.

There will no longer be any curse; and the throne of God and of the Lamb will be in it, and His bond-servants will serve Him; they will see His face, and His name *will be* on their foreheads.

And there will no longer be *any* night; and they will not have need of the light of a lamp nor the light of the sun, because the Lord God will illumine them; and they will reign forever and ever."

The eternal glory of the Lord is available to anyone who whole-heartedly accepts His free gift of eternal salvation, as long as it is before we take our last and final breath. Scripture tells us there will be "multitudes" that will wait until they find themselves living through the inescapable terrors of the Tribulation to accept Christ's free gift of salvation. Please don't wait. Tomorrow is promised to no one. Any one of us could take our last breath today. Then it will be too late. The only way we can embrace righteousness and holiness is to be covered by the atoning blood sacrifice of Jesus. And in conclusion, John leaves us with some final messages:

"And he said to me, "These words are faithful and true"; and the Lord, the God of the spirits of the prophets, sent His angel to show to His bond-servants the things which must soon take place" (Revelation 22:6).

"I, John, am the one who heard and saw these things. And when I heard and saw, I fell down to worship at the feet of the angel who showed me these things. But he said to me, "Do not do that. I am a fellow servant of yours and of your brethren the prophets and of those who heed the words of this book. Worship God" (Revelation 22:8).

"I, Jesus have sent My angel to testify to you these things for the churches, I am the Root and the Offspring of David, the Bright and Morning Star" (Revelation 22:16).

Chapter Nineteen

How Do We Worship the Lord?

Worshipping the Lord is expressed in many different ways and under various circumstances. We can worship the Lord by playing musical instruments, singing, clapping, bowing, standing, dancing, lifting our hands, or by praising the Lord with endearing words. Giving to others is a form of worship because when we give with a loving and generous heart we are honoring the Lord by caring for others. Sometimes in group-settings or alone, we worship aloud but not in a manner or intent that will draw attention to ourselves. We should always direct our attention to the glory to God. By reading these Psalms, we can see many ways to worship:

"And now my head shall be lifted up above my enemies all around me; therefore I will offer sacrifices of joy in His tabernacle; I will sing, yes, I will sing praises of the LORD" (Psalm 27:6).

"Praise the Lord with the harp; make music to Him with an instrument of ten strings" (Psalm 33:2).

"Sing to Him a new song; play skillfully with a shout of joy" (Psalm 33:3).

"I will bless the LORD at all times; His praise *shall* continually *be* in my mouth" (Psalm 4:1).

"Sing praises to God, sing praises to our King, sing praises" (Psalm 47:6).

"OH, clap your hands, all you peoples! Shout to God with the voice of triumph" (Psalm 47:1).

Thus I will praise You while I live, and in your name I will lift up my hands in Your name. (Psalm 63:4)

"OH come, let us sing to the LORD! Let us shout joyfully to the Rock of our salvation, let us come before His presence with thanksgiving; let us shout joyfully to Him with psalms" (Psalm 95:1-2).

"Oh come, let us worship and bow down, let us kneel before the LORD our Maker" (Psalm 95:6).

"Let them praise his name with the dance; let them sing praises to Him with the timbrel and harp" (Psalm 149:3).

❧ Glossary ❧

Angels - Created beings, those who serve God and serve born-again believers. One third of them (fallen angels) joined Satan when he rebelled against God. In the Bible angels always appear in the male gender. We are never to worship angels—worship only God (Revelation 22:8-9).

Antichrist - Antichrist is the name given to the man referred to in the Bible as the "Man of Sin" or the "Beast." He is a man, who will be indwelt and empowered by Satan halfway through the Tribulation. He will rise to power in the last days and ruthlessly persecute people, especially the Jews during the Tribulation. When Jesus returns, he will destroy the Antichrist, casting him into the lake of fire where he will also cast Satan.

After the Rapture he will assume control of the world, but he will be under the power of the world church (Revelation 17:3). At the mid-point of the seven-year Tribulation he will take total control of earth by the power of Satan (Revelation 13:4) and rule with absolute authority for 42 months (Revelation 13.5). He will blaspheme God (Daniel 7:25; Revelation 13:5-6) and persecute and kill those who are saved after the Rapture (Daniel 7:21, 25; Revelation 13:7)

Apologetics - Simply defined, it is the defense of the Christian faith.

Apostasy - In the *Holman Illustrated Bible Dictionary*, the first definition for "apostasy" is: Act of rebelling against, forsaking, abandoning, or falling away from what one has formerly believed. The English word "apostasy" is derived from a Greek word (apostasia) which means, "to stand away from." In Thessalonians 2:3, Scripture teaches that the explosion of false doctrines in the last days will take hold, making the way for Antichrist. The following verse clearly shows that some will teach false doctrines and *many will be deceived* by prominent, popular, accepted teachings that are really false teachings that contradict the true teachings of the Bible adding to the apostasy.

> "Now the spirit expressly says that in latter times some will depart from the faith, giving heed to deceiving spirits and doctrines of demons, speaking lies in hypocrisy, having their own conscience seared with a hot iron" (1 Timothy 4:1-2).

Apostles - The eleven disciples who were chosen by Jesus to go forth and preach the gospel. (Matthew 28:19-20, Luke 1:26, Acts 1:8, Ephesians 4:11-13).

Archangel - A chief angel, in the New Testament there is reference to: Michael the archangel.

Atheism - Atheism is the belief that God does not exist. Atheists believe that there is no God.

Baptism - The word "baptism" refers to the act of being placed into or "immersed" into something. New believers are "baptized" into water to symbolize the fact that we are dead and "buried" to an old way of life; that Jesus died and was buried in the tomb before He came back to life. Baptism is a testimony to the world of our commitment to Messiah Jesus and as an act of obedience to our Lord.

Beast - The Beast is the Antichrist. He is the future world leader who is also called the man of sin and son of perdition among other names (2 Thessalonians 2:3). Some people mistakenly teach the Catholic Church is the Beast, but that is not true.

Believer (Christian) - This term is used by some individuals, instead of the word "Christian." It is a term often used by Jewish followers of Yeshua (Jesus). The term "believer" is in reference to one who genuinely believes in Yeshua Ha Mashiach (Jesus the Christ) and is saved by faith; a "born-again" individual.

Born-again - The Bible teaches that when we receive Jesus Christ into our lives as our Lord and Savior, our lives are changed reflecting God's will for our lives and we are so different that we can be called "new creatures." To emphasize this total change in our lives, Messiah Jesus called the transformation "born-again." A true Christian or believer is "born-again" (John 3:7).

"Jesus answered and said unto him, 'Most assuredly, I say to you, unless one is born-again he cannot see the kingdom of God'" (John 3:3). "Do not marvel that I said to you, you must be born-again" (John 3:7). Having been born-again, not of corruptible seed but of incorruptible, through the word of God, which lives and abides forever" (1 Peter 1:23).

Cherubim - Cherubim/cherubs are angelic beings involved in the worship and praise of God; winged creatures (Genesis 3:24).

Christ - His full name and title is the Lord Jesus Christ. The word "Christ is" "Messiah" in Hebrew. He is *the* anointed or specially chosen One of God. He is anointed, or specially chosen, to bring salvation to mankind by His death on the cross.

Church - The church is the body of Christ, which consists of all true born-again believers in Jesus (1 Corinthians 12.27; Ephesians 4:12).

Communion - Communion is a special name for the "Lord's Supper." The word "communion" emphasizes the personal relationship and fellowship we have with the Lord Jesus Christ and with others believers.

Conversion - This word refers to the total change that takes place when we receive the Lord Jesus Christ into our lives and genuinely give ourselves to Him.

Conviction - The word "conviction" is most often used when we have behaved in ways that are wrong, and the Holy Spirit reminds us that we have sinned. We express that by saying that we are "under conviction." People who have never received the Lord Jesus Christ as their personal Lord and Savior sometimes fight "conviction" for a long time before they finally repent and truly surrender to the Lord and begin to process of renewing their minds.

True believers will hopefully learn to repent quickly when the Holy Spirit brings conviction. The word "conviction" is also used to refer to our strong beliefs upon which we base our lives, our belief in the Bible as the complete inerrant Word of God. As Christians/believers we have many strong convictions that we know to be to be true. An example: We have an absolute conviction that Messiah Jesus rose from the dead, and will return at the end of the Tribulation in the Second Advent.

Cult - A cult is a group of people who claim to believe the Bible and even claim to believe in the Lord Jesus Christ. But their actual teachings are so far off from what the Bible truly teaches that the group members (the cult) are not true Christians or believers; but they think they are.

Some examples would be those who do not believe that Jesus Christ is really God, or those who believe that salvation can be attained in some way besides faith in Messiah Jesus. A cult can also consist of persons who have concocted their own "spiritual" teachings, and the Bible is rendered just another "holy" book.

Day of Christ - The same as the Day of the Lord. It is a period of time that begins with the Rapture/Tribulation and ends at the Second Coming of Jesus Christ.

Denomination - A denomination is a Christian group that believes and practices things slightly differently from other Christian groups. Individual churches are often part of a larger denomination. However, all Christian denominations agree that the Lord Jesus Christ is God who became man in order to die for our sins, and that faith and acceptance of Him is the only way to receive eternal life.

Disciple - An individual believing in and following all the teachings and truth of Messiah Jesus.

Disciples - (twelve disciples) - The twelve men Jesus chose (His inner circle) and were taught by Him (Luke 6:13-16) in order that they could build His church after His ascension. These same men became the apostles, excluding Judas Iscariot who betrayed Jesus.

Doctrine - Doctrine is a term referring to the teachings and principles that are taught in the Bible.

Elect - Christians/believers are called "the elect." Not because they are special or better than anyone else, but because they have placed their faith in the saving grace of Messiah Jesus. The word "elect" found in Scripture is also in relation to a specific prophesied events and groups of people:

In Matthew 24:22 the reference to the elect are mostly Jews who flee from the Antichrist when his image is set up in the newly built temple in Jerusalem halfway through the Tribulation. There will be many Gentiles also in that group.

A good number of them will have believed in Jesus as their Savior and will be saved during the first half of the Tribulation.

In the middle of the Tribulation, they will have to flee for their lives (Matthew 24:16- 22; Revelation 12).

Also the Tribulation saints of Revelation 20:4 who die during the fifth and sixth seals (Revelation 6:9-11, 12-16) and go to heaven as shown in (Revelation 7:9-17) are another group of "elect." But they are not the elect of Matthew 24:31; 25:31-34.

For those Jews and Gentiles are the saints (the elect) who do not die during the Tribulation. They will survive the Tribulation and will be **alive** when Jesus the Messiah returns to earth (Revelation 19:11), and they are the sheep who enter the millennial kingdom in Matthew 25:34.

Emmanuel /Immanuel - means "God with us" in Hebrew.

End Times - An indeterminate period of time that began with the "falling away" (Apostasy) of the church and will end with the Second Coming of Jesus Christ. We are living in the End Times, also referred to as the last days.

Epistle - An *epistle* simply means a letter (as in written correspondence). The epistles of the New Testament follow the form for letters in the first century. Letters in those days were not placed in envelopes, so they began with the name of the sender, followed by the name of the recipient, and then a greeting. However, the Epistle to the Hebrews did not follow this particular style.

Eschatology - The study of the "last things" in the Bible. The "last things" are also known as the End Times and the Last Days.

Evangelism - Evangelism generally means sharing the good news about Jesus Christ. This can be done one-on-one (person to person). It can also be done in large, group "evangelistic" meetings. Doing the work of evangelism means telling others about what Jesus has done for them, providing them an opportunity to receive Jesus Christ as their personal Lord and Savior.

Faith - Faith is more than "head knowledge" about the truth of Jesus Christ. Faith means putting our complete trust in Jesus Christ, and in Him alone, to save us from sin, death, and hell.

False Prophet - The religious leader who will head up the coming world church; he enforces the Antichrist's dictates working closely with him (Revelation 13:11-18).

Fundamentalist - The word "fundamentalist" has a number of meanings. Most often, individuals use it to refer to people of any denomination that believe that the Bible is the Word of God, completely true in all of its parts and totally without error.

Gospel - "Gospel" literally means "good news." It refers to the good news that Jesus Christ, God the Son, became a man like us. He lived a perfect and sinless life. He died on the cross to pay the penalty for our sins. He rose again and lives forever. He will forgive our sin and give us eternal life when we truly repent and place our faith in Him.

Grace - God offers us His Grace (unmerited favor) by freely giving us the gifts of forgiveness, righteousness, eternal life, peace, joy, and things that we cannot yet fully understand here in our earthly state.

Heaven - The Word of God—the Bible, teaches us that heaven is a phenomenal, perfect place that exists in the spirit world. It is the place where God and His holy angels dwell. It is a place where continual, never-ending worship of God takes place. When all true believers die, their spirits go to heaven.

Hell - God's Word tells us that those who reject God's gift of Eternal Life through Messiah Jesus will go to a horrific place called hell. Hell was prepared for Satan and his angels. It is a place of incomprehensible torment.

But God has provided a way for mankind to stay out of hell. By receiving Messiah Jesus as our personal Lord and Savior, He gives us the gift of eternal life and victory over Satan's plan to deceive us and keep us from the true God of the Bible.

Heresy - Heresy refers to serious errors in what people believe. So serious, individuals who believe those things cannot really be Christians/Believers. A good example of heresy is to believe that Jesus Christ or the Holy Spirit is not truly God. It is a heresy to believe that there is some other way to be saved from our sins other than faith in the Messiah Jesus. It is absolute heresy to believe that Jesus Christ (Yeshua) did not really die for our sins, or that He did not rise from the dead.

Holy Spirit - The Holy Spirit is God. He is the third person of the Trinity. As God, He is Omniscient, Omnipresent, and Omnipotent. He comes to live inside us when we genuinely repent and receive Messiah Jesus as our personal Lord and Savior. The Holy Spirit gives us direction and wisdom for making life's decisions as we make the Lord the priority of our lives and as we learn to listen to His voice.

Hypocrisy - Hypocrisy means "pretense." People who claim to be living for Christ but who are really not living for Christ are filled with of hypocrisy. They are hypocrites.

Incarnation - The incarnation is in reference to the time when God (who is Spirit) became a man. This occurred when Jesus (God the Son) was conceived by God the Father by means of God the Holy Spirit in the womb of the young Jewish woman, Mary.

Indwelling of the Holy Spirit - When we truly repent and receive Messiah Jesus as our Lord and Savior, the Holy Spirit of God comes to live inside us. He never leaves us again. The Holy Spirit lives or dwells within us forever (John 14:16).

Inerrancy - The belief that God purposed His Word, the Bible, to be written perfectly and without any errors at all.

Infallible - Infallible is similar to the word "inerrant." Since the Bible is God's perfect Word, it cannot fail or mislead us in any way. It is perfect and complete.

Lake of Fire - The final abode of Satan and the fallen angels (Matthew 25:41; Revelation 20:10). It is also the final abode of everyone who dies in their sins without trusting in Jesus Christ to save them (Revelation 20:11-15). Everyone who is cast into that place of punishment (Proverbs 10:16; Matthew 25:46) has no hope of parole, pardon or escape!

Lost - Before we receive the Lord Jesus Christ as our personal Lord and Savior, we are said to be "lost." After we receive the Lord Jesus Christ we are "saved." Lost people do not have their sins forgiven until they truly repent and receive Christ.

Maranatha - "Our Lord comes," or is "coming" (1 Corinthians 16:22).

Mark of the Beast - A mark of some kind (some think it will be a computer chip implanted under the skin) that the Antichrist will force everyone on earth to take to be able to buy or sell or receive any kind of government benefits. Those who refuse to worship the Antichrist and take his mark will be executed (Revelation 13:15-17).

Messiah - The word "Messiah" comes from the Hebrew word that is translated by the Greek word that means "Christ." Jesus Christ is the Messiah spoken of in Scripture. See Isaiah 53. *Messiah* is derived from the Hebrew word: *Mashiach* ("Anointed One").

Millennial Kingdom - The period of time that begins with the Second Coming of Jesus Christ and ends after 1,000 years

(Revelation 20:1-10). It is also called the Millennium. The major passages describing that age are – Isaiah 4:1-6; 11.6-10; 25:6-7; 60:1-9; 61:3-11; 62:1-9; 65:17-25; 66:22-24; Jeremiah 23:3-8; 30:18-22; 33:6-18; Ezekiel 40-48; Joel 3:18-21; Micah 4:1-8; Zephaniah 3:9-13; Zechariah 14:9-11, 16-21.

New Testament - The second part of the Bible, B'rit Hadashah in Hebrew.

Old Testament - The first section of the Bible, the Tenakh.

Olivet Discourse - Shortly before Messiah Jesus was arrested He spoke with His twelve disciples about future developments and circumstances. This is noted in Matthew 24-25, Mark 13 and Luke 21.

Omnipotent - Omnipotent means "all powerful." It is a word that describes God, and God alone. He has perfect and total power in the entire universe. He has the power to do anything He chooses to do.

Omnipresent - Omnipresent means that God can be everywhere, and at the same time. Wherever we go, whatever we do, God is there with us all the time. At the same time He is everywhere else with everyone else. Only God is Omnipresent.

Omniscience - Omniscience means that God knows everything, every detail. He has all knowledge. There is nothing hidden from Him. He knows every bit of information about you and me and everyone else on earth as well as every single aspect of the entire universe. We can't hide from God.

Pantheism - Pantheism is the belief that creation (nature) is God. Pantheists believe that the rocks, mountains, earth, stars, etc. are all part of God. Christians, however, believe that God *made all these things.* Although Christians believe God is omnipresent, they believe God is totally separate from *His Creation.*

Passover - Passover is part of the feast of unleavened bread, commemorating the epic Exodus when God's covenant people were delivered from Egyptian bondage. On the 14th day of Nisan the sacrificial lamb (animal) was slain. The blood of atonement upon the doorpost (in the form of a cross) brought salvation as the death angel passed overhead, on the eve of Passover. This was the Old Covenant fulfillment of Passover for *national protection,* and deliverance from the death angel. On the 14th day of Nisan in 30 A.D. on the eve of Passover, Messiah Jesus was crucified

The blood of the promised Sacrificial Lamb was shed. This was the redemption God provided. It brings salvation to His covenant people delivering them from the bondage of sin and death. This is the New Covenant fulfillment of Passover for personal salvation. Salvation comes by the atoning blood of Israel's promised Sacrificial Lamb (Jesus). The apostle Paul called Christ "our Passover" (1 Corinthians 5:7). Also see Isaiah 53 in the Bible.

Pentecost - The official day that the church began (Acts 2:1). On that day 120 believers in Jesus Christ gathered to pray (Acts

1:12-15). The Holy Spirit came and took up residence inside of them (Acts 2:1-4). The Disciples then went out and preached the gospel (Acts 2:5-13). Peter gave the concluding sermon (Acts 2:14-40), and about three thousand people were saved on that glorious day (Acts 2:41).

Rapture - The snatching off the planet of all believers in Jesus Christ (1 Thessalonians 4:16-17). It takes place before the Tribulation starts. The Pre-Tribulation Rapture teaches Jesus Christ will rapture the church prior to the start of the Tribulation.

Pre-Tribulation Rapture teaches Jesus Christ will rapture the church before the start of the Tribulation.

Mid-Tribulation Rapture teaches Jesus Christ will rapture the church at the mid-point of the Tribulation.

Post-Tribulation Rapture teaches Jesus Christ will rapture the church at the end of the Tribulation.

Pre-Wrath Rapture teaches Jesus Christ will rapture the church near the end of the Tribulation just before the pouring out of the wrath of God through the seven bowl plagues (Revelation 16:1).

Reconciliation - Since God is completely holy and since men are sinners, there is a separation, a gap between men and God. Sin separates us from God. Messiah Jesus paid the death penalty for our sin, making it possible for us to be forgiven and cleansed of sin, bringing man and God together by taking away man's sin.

Rededication - Sometimes Christians realize that they have not been really committed to the Lord, and are living their lives in such a way that they grieve the Holy Spirit. When God convicts them that they have been making poor choices contrary to His teachings, they should and need to "rededicate" or renew their commitment to Him. This is done by asking for forgiveness and starting again with a truly repented heart and attitude.

Redeemed - When Messiah Jesus died on the cross; He paid the price for our sin. He purchased us from Satan. We are "redeemed" when we receive Him as or Lord and Savior.

Resurrection - Resurrection means to come back to life in such a way as to live forever and never die again. After His death and burial, the Lord Jesus Christ experienced resurrection. He literally came back to life and He lives forever and ever.

Ru Ha Kodesh - Is Holy Spirit in Hebrew.

Satan - Satan was once one of the greatest angels ever created by God; also known as Lucifer, and the devil. He became full of pride and self-adulation and rebelled against God. He was the highest-ranking angel who led a rebellion of angels taking one-third of them with him (Revelation 12:4).

He is the ruler (John 12:31) and the god of this world (2 Corinthians 4:4). He is also the leader of all the forces of darkness (Ephesians 6:12). All believers know that Satan was ultimately defeated when Jesus died on the cross, and will not win His war against God.

Saved - A very popular word describing truly born-again Christians/Believers is the word "saved." When we receive the Lord Jesus Christ, He "saves" us from the ravages of sin, death, and hell. We are "saved" and will not suffer the coming Tribulation or hell. We have eternal life through Him.

Second Coming - The physical and literal return of Jesus Christ to earth (Matthew 25:31-46; Revelation19:11-21).   After His return He establishes the Millennial Kingdom. It is also referred to as the Second Advent and the Glorious Appearing.

Security of the Believer - When we receive the Lord Jesus Christ as our Savior and truly repent, He promises to keep us forever. He promises that nothing can ever separate us from His love or take us out of His hand. We are secure forever in Him. No matter what happens to us in this life, we can be confident that Messiah Jesus will never leave us. We can be confident that when we die, we will be with Him forever, for eternity.

Seraphim - Seraphim are creatures with six wings, particularly focused on continually worshipping God (Isaiah 6:2-4).

Shabbat - This is the Hebrew word for "ceasing" or "stopping." This word is also used for the seventh day, the Shabbat; the day work stops (7th day of the week) to rest and contemplate on the Lord. "For six days work may be done; but on the seventh day there is a Sabbath of complete rest, a holy convocation. You shall not do any work; it is a Sabbath to the LORD in all your dwelling" (Leviticus 23:3).

Shalom - The Hebrew word for peace and God's blessing; used as a greeting.

Sin - Sin means, "To miss the mark." The Lord has told us in the Bible how we should live our lives. His holy Word is a guideline for our lives. But without a doubt, we have all gone against His Ten Commandments. We have all sinned. The more we live according to God's commandments, the more peace we will have. But none of us can "fix" our sin problems by just *trying* to be good. That is why the Lord Jesus Christ died on the cross, to pay the death penalty for our sins in our place.

Temptation - Temptation is when our minds tell is it is okay to do something that God clearly tells us is sin. We are all tempted, even Jesus was tempted. We can choose to do the right thing and win over temptation by keeping the Word of God close to our hearts, and always praying for strength to overcome temptations.

Trinity - The Bible teaches that God reveals Himself as One God Who exists as three *persons*: God the Father, God the Son, and God the Holy Spirit. The word "Trinity" combines the prefix "tri" meaning "three." with the word "unity" which means "one."

Walking in the flesh - Walking in the flesh means living one's life continually succumbing to temptations leading to a life filled with sin.

Walking in the Spirit - living our lives in a way that reflects the inner workings of the Holy Spirit dwelling within all true believers.

Yahweh - A Hebrew word for God.

Yeshua - Jesus in the name of the Messiah. Yeshua is a Hebrew word that has the root meaning: salvation (Matthew 1:18-21).

Yeshua Ha Mashiach - Jesus the Christ: in Hebrew.

Important Resources

The best way to locate the suggested material is by searching the Internet by book or DVD title. Your local bookstore may carry a number of these items. At the time of this publication the websites are current, but may be subject to change.

Website Especially for Youth

Good stuff! A must see website for all teens is cited below. It includes multiple topics relating to *all* social issues ranging from peer pressure, dating, depression, emotional and physical abuse, addiction, emotions, friendships, jobs, God and much, much more. This link is part of (christiananswers.net), but specifically linked here for youth:

http://www.christiananswers.net/teens/home.html.

God in My Corner - A Spiritual Memoir by George Forman, with Ken Abraham - Inspiring, encouraging and motivational; how God became number one for the former Olympic gold medalist, two-time heavyweight world boxing champion, turned pastor (very involved with young people).

Hath God Said? - Eric Barger - Why the Bible is reliable, inspired and infallible. Anyone in doubt about the truth of God's Word should read this book.

Entertaining Spirits Unaware: The End Times Occult Invasion- David Benoit and Eric Barger - book or DVD format – This site has excellent detailed biblical information concerning the Modern Witchcraft Movement, Necromancy, Channelers, Psychics, Magic. Especially important for parents, a must-read for everyone, and why EVERY parent should be concerned about Harry Potter. Included are the dangers of occult themed entertainment promotions (Yu-Gi-Oh, Pokémon, Halloween, UFOs, Harry Potter, and more). Good information on the rise of the Cult of Relativism.

Hidden Dangers in Harry Potter - DVD - Steve Wohlberg.

Harry Potter: Witchcraft Repackaged: Making Evil Look Innocent DVD by Caryl Productions.

Disarming the Powers of Darkness: What Every Christian Parent Needs to Know About the Occult - DVD - David Benoit.

Faith Undone, Roger Oakland - Exposing the dangers of the emergent church movement grounded in age-old mystical approach; a highly deceptive teaching leading to Roman Catholicism and interfaith perspectives -- pointing toward the coming One World ecumenical religious system of Revelation 17.

Queen of All: The Marian Apparitions' Plan to Unite all Religions under the Roman Catholic Church - Jim Tetlow and Roger Oakland

The Death of Discernment: How The Shack became the #1 Bestseller in Christianity - Eric Barger - This is an extremely important expose of how unbiblical doctrines contained in the best seller, *The Shack* has deceived countless numbers of Christians and seekers of truth. *The Shack* marks an unparalleled lack of discernment within Christianity.

Bringing Twilight Out into the Son, by Eric Barger - A quick-read booklet. As the author, Eric Barger explains: "Blockbuster books and hit movies confuse evil with good. You may know someone who is in love with the *Twilight* books by Mormon author, Stephenie Meyer. These books and the resulting movies have helped to induce a disturbing acceptance of vampirism among teenagers - especially teen girls. Also, as with many storylines today, the *Twilight* series endears readers and viewers to heroes who are, in reality, villainous. In short, this extremely popular saga is desensitizing millions concerning the satanic underworld.

A Twist of Faith - Berit Kjos - Especially good for women involved in the Goddess, feminist myths that have replaced biblical facts.

Evidence the Bible Is True from Archeology, Science and Prophecy - CD Rom - Roger Oakland.

Global Warming: A Scientific and Biblical Expose of Climate Change DVD - Dr. Larry Vardiman, and many other scientists. This is an excellent presentation addressing the distortions behind the Global Warming agenda.

Universalism: Is Everyone Already Saved? Eric Barger shows why the biblical truths of salvation through Jesus Christ alone, the absolute need for a regenerating, "born-again" experience, and the fact that eternal and unending separation from God awaits all, who reject salvation through Jesus Christ's sacrificial death.

Is Your Church New Age, Emergent of Christian? Eric Barger Explore the differences in doctrine and theology of the different types of so-called Christian churches in the United States today, some of which are Christian in name only (DVD or CD).

The Real Jesus vs. the Counterfeits - Eric Barger - An excellent teaching on how religions/cults outside the true teachings of the Bible speak about a "Jesus" that is not the real Jesus of the Bible, but rather *a counterfeit Jesus.* Many, sincere, good people are deceived by the imposters. Those following a "different Jesus" are without a Savior (Jesus Christ) and are headed for an eternal torment.

Seeing God Through the Human Body: A Doctor's Meditation on the Human Miracle - Dr. Robert Peprah-Gyamfi.

www.christiananswers.net - An outstanding website providing biblical answers to contemporary questions for all ages and nationalities containing over forty-five thousand files with valuable information on personal issues, social issues, Bible topics, world religions, children's section, online entertainment and movies, streaming videos; movie and video reviews. Also includes an online store with products available in multilingual formats.

www.ericbarger.com - Eric Barger's, Take A Stand Ministries - Downloads available - An online store with great must-have DVDs, CDs and books. This is an outstanding website loaded with vital information on Cults, Spiritual Warfare, Halloween, The New Age Movement, The Occult and Witchcraft (including Harry Potter and The Lord of the Rings), Today's Music and Entertainment, Environmentalism, Troubling Trends in the church and Prophecy, Globalism, Roman Catholicism, and more.

http://home.earthlink.net/~ronrhodes/Downloadable.html. Dr. Ron Rhodes, *Reasoning from the Scriptures Ministry*: Excellent, must-read information on important very current, topics very relevant today: Recovering from the Recovery Movement, Is Reincarnation Biblical? Close Encounters of the Celestial Kind, Evaluating Today's Angel Craze, Confusion in Christian Music, The Debate over Feminist Theology and much more. Thoroughly research this entire website. You will also find a list of some exceptional, must-read books by Dr. Rhodes.

http://www.justforcatholics.org/ - A great website, especially good for Catholics with the focus on salvation and other Catholic-related issues; also good for Protestants.

http://www.religiouscounterfeits.org/nas.htm - Interesting, very informative site on religious counterfeits and New Age deception, including the Catholic connection to the New Age god of pantheism.

http://worldviewweekend.com/ - Brannon Howse, president and founder of *Worldview Weekend Foundation* - Interesting, excellent website packed with very important information: Radio, video, television, commentaries, music, interviews and bookstore. The focus is on spiritual discernment, biblical integrity and world socio-economic issues.

The Case for Jesus the Messiah—Incredible Prophecies that Prove God Exists by Dr. John Ankerberg and Dr. John Weldon. This 25 part teaching (PDF) is filled with undeniable evidence for the truth of Yeshua, the Messiah. Be sure to visit http://www.jashow.org/wiki/index.php?title=The_Case_for_Jesus_the_Messiah_-_Incredible_Prophecies_that_Prove_God_Exists

http://www.livingwaters.com/ - Evangelist, Ray Comfort. Excellent website packed with good information and resources.

http://www.ccgreenvalley.org/default.aspx - Senior Pastor John Knapp, Calvary Chapel Green Valley. This is a recommendation to view and/or carefully listen to the entire book of Romans teaching in the New Testament section to gain an excellent understanding of the sin nature and salvation through Christ and Christ alone.

Disclaimer: Although the resources listed are generally excellent, Friends of Yeshua Ministries does not agree with every single point on every topic taught and posted on the recommended websites, so please check your Bible to be sure what is being presented is in keeping with the Scriptures (Acts 17:11).

God Created Everything

"The earth is full of the goodness of the LORD. By the word of the LORD the heavens were made and the host of them by the breath of His mouth. Let all the inhabitants of the world stand in awe of Him. For He spoke, and it was done; He commanded, and it stood fast" (Psalm 33:5b-6; 8b-9).

"Thus says the LORD, the Holy One of Israel, and His Maker; I have made the earth and created man on it. I – My hands – stretched out the heavens, and all their host I have commanded" (Isaiah 45:11a, 12).

Evidence for the Truth
❧ of Biblical Creation ❧

Dr. David Hocking - An excellent teaching on Creation and the myth of Evolution: *Genesis DVDs are* available through his website at: http://www.davidhocking.org/ or call 1-800-752-4253.

God of Wonders DVD - This amazing DVD takes us through the creation story and the gospel with spectacular photography, and tremendous facts about God's handiwork in creation including the examination of the incredible complexity of DNA: http://www.christiancinema.com/downloads/GodWonders.pdf

Without Form and Void - A Study of the Meaning of Genesis - Arthur Custance. In this scholarly analysis, Dr. Custance observes the rules of linguistics, of grammar and syntax, and also examines how words are used in the rest of Scripture. In this book, Dr. Custance demonstrates to the reader that there *can be* a gap in time between Genesis 1:1 and 1:2, a gap that allows for an ancient earth, and the recent creation of humankind. Please visit the website which contains the works of Arthur Custance (1910-1985), showcasing his vision to bring together the established facts of Science and the revealed truths of Scripture. http://www.custance.org/.

Place Your Trust in the Lord

Psalm 5:11-12

"But let all those rejoice who put their trust in You; let them ever shout for joy, because You defend them; let those also who love Your name be joyful in You. But You, O LORD, will bless the righteous; with favor You will surround him as with a shield."

✌ Acknowledgments ✍

The words, Rapture and Todd Strandberg, are nearly synonymous. I cannot mention the word Rapture without Todd coming to mind. He is strongly dedicated to spreading the Pre-Tribulation Rapture and salvation message via the Internet. Todd is my colleague and co-laborer for Christ (as he puts it) and sole founder of Rapture Ready. As early as the 1980s on his first computer, Todd had already laid the groundwork for what would become Rapture Ready as we know it today. Working with him is a daily adventure as we grow the site to reach others. His foresight, dedication and steadfastness to get the gospel out into the world has touched millions of lives.

Another special person is my friend, David Chagall. He and his wonderful wife, Juneau, were instrumental in my walk with Christ after my rededication to Him—soon after the Holy Spirit intervened in my life in a New Age bookstore in Virginia—bringing me back to the faith after a long sojourn away. David is the first person, whom I ever heard mention the topic of the Rapture (although, I had attended a number of Christian churches for many years). I will never forget when we were about to end our telephone conversation the first time we spoke. He said, "We'll talk to you soon or we'll see you in the air." I didn't have a clue what he was talking about at the time: "We'll see you in the air?"

I must also mention Dr. F. Kenton Beshore (Doc), Mrs. Lois Beshore and the staff at the World Bible Society. Dr. Beshore's incredible scholarship is far beyond the hyped-up talk you hear from many who love to stand in the limelight and have themselves elevated above others. At a time when so many are clamoring for worldly recognition (fame and fortune), and are undeservedly called prophecy "experts" and even "scholars," Doc Beshore is in a different league all together. He really is an expert, a brilliant scholar who is not self-seeking, never displaying a condescending attitude, always treating others with respect.

His knowledge and expertise are unsurpassed when it comes to understanding and teaching the Word of God. You have not been to a lecture until you have heard Dr. Beshore deliver the Word of God with his thorough detailed intricate exposition. Our relationship is very special and I am blessed to have such a learned, unassuming man as my strong advocate. His staff is always so gracious, going the extra-mile on my behalf. Thank you for standing behind me with the publishing of my books. God bless all of you.

I also wish to reflect upon my dear friend, Terry Nasca. I am so grateful for our lifelong friendship. We met when I could barely speak a few words of English—when we were young children, and today we are still strong friends, and best of all—sisters in the Lord. Her loyal steadfast encouragement, regarding this book especially, has been a tremendous blessing.

⌒ About the Author ⌒

Kit Olsen is a Christian author, also specializing in Christian book editing and ghostwriting for multinational publishers and ministries. She is currently the General Editor for Rapture Ready, the number one Christian prophecy website in the world, and has written hundreds of articles (FAQs) as a staff writer for the site. Her weekly column on Rapture Ready, "Dear Esther," is a fresh insightful biblical alternative to secular advice columns, providing wise counsel to those who are in need of guidance, comfort and encouragement.

Kit has been involved in evangelism using the written word since 1995. Her magazine—Southern Nevada Christian Review—a successful witnessing venture was her first Christian publication. She worked for many years as researcher, writer, editor, and media representative for a Hebrew-Christian television ministry.

She is experienced in audiovisual production, media photography, varied forms of writing including music and accompanying lyrics; editing, design and layout of advertising material, media graphics, marketing. Born in Austria, Kit has traveled and worked extensively all around the world and has a small outreach ministry, Friends of Yeshua Ministries.

Prior to working primarily with the Christian community Kit began writing and editing professionally while still a senior in college as an editor for the National Institutes of Health editing medical protocols, and later writing copy for Meredith Enterprises, on Madison Avenue. She also wrote and produced documentary slideshows for the State of New York before moving on to various other media communications work.

Her previously published books by the World Bible Society are: *A Better World Is Coming Soon - Don't Miss It* (2011). And more recently, *A Better World Is Coming Soon - Don't Miss It* (Expanded 2013 Edition)—an exceptional book on Bible prophecy; an eschatological anthology which also documents her personal testimony about how she came to salvation in Christ after a long struggle to find authenticity in a world of deceit, corruption and compromise—ultimately walking away from a blossoming career in the entertainment industry, unable to reconcile the moral depravity that is especially prevalent in the world of Arts and Entertainment—choosing instead to serve Christ (Joshua 24:16; John 12:26).

NOTES

Olsen, Kit: *A Better World Is Coming Soon – Don't Miss It,* World Bible Society, February 2013 Expanded Edition. Throughout this book a small amount of previously published material written by the author is added and slightly modified as it is relevant and applicable to the subject matter.

Numbers 6:24-26

"The LORD bless you and keep you; the LORD make His face shine upon you, and be gracious to you; the LORD lift up His countenance upon you, and give you peace."

Made in the USA
Lexington, KY
28 July 2014